Operations Management in Services

Abhishek Sharma
Manish Sharma

ACKNOWLEDGEMENT

We would like to thank our families and our colleagues for their steady support and encouragement

CONTENTS

CHAPTER 1

Role of Services in an Economy

Services play a crucial role in an economy and are a fundamental component of economic activity. While goods are tangible products that can be manufactured and traded, services are intangible activities or performances that are provided to fulfill a need or desire. Here are some key roles that services play in an economy:

1. Job Creation: The service sector often serves as a major source of employment in modern economies. Services encompass a wide range of industries such as healthcare, education, finance, transportation, hospitality, and professional services. These sectors create job opportunities, which contribute to economic growth, reduce unemployment, and improve living standards.

2. Economic Growth: Services can be significant drivers of economic growth. As the service sector expands, it generates income and stimulates demand, leading to increased consumption and production. Services often have high value-added components, which contribute to productivity improvements and overall economic development.

3. Innovation and Technological Advancement: Services frequently involve innovation and the application of new technologies. Advancements in information technology, telecommunications, financial services, and digital platforms have revolutionized the way services are delivered and

consumed. Technological innovation in services can enhance productivity, efficiency, and customer experiences, leading to improved economic performance.

4. Diversification of the Economy: Services provide diversification opportunities for economies heavily reliant on traditional industries such as agriculture or manufacturing. Developing a robust service sector can reduce dependence on a single industry, making the economy more resilient to external shocks and global market fluctuations.

5. Trade and Globalization: Services play a vital role in international trade. Cross-border trade in services, known as the export or import of services, has become increasingly significant. This includes sectors like tourism, financial services, telecommunications, and business services. Services trade promotes economic integration, enhances competitiveness, and fosters global cooperation.

6. Consumer Welfare: Services directly contribute to consumer welfare and quality of life. Services such as healthcare, education, entertainment, and leisure activities are essential for societal well-being. Improvements in the quality, accessibility, and affordability of services can lead to better standards of living and improved social outcomes.

7. Interconnectedness with Other Sectors: Services are closely linked to other sectors of the economy. Many goods-producing industries rely on a range of services, including logistics, marketing, legal, and financial services. The performance of the service sector has a ripple effect on the entire economy, influencing productivity, competitiveness, and economic stability.

Service Definitions

Services: Services refer to intangible economic activities or performances that are offered to fulfill a need or desire. They are typically provided by one party to another and can involve a wide range of activities such as professional advice, expertise, assistance, or the provision of experiences.

Service Sector: The service sector, also known as the tertiary sector, is a broad category that encompasses industries involved in the production and delivery of services. It includes sectors such as healthcare, education, finance, hospitality, transportation, communication, professional services, and entertainment.

Service Economy: A service economy refers to an economic system where the majority of economic activity and employment is concentrated in the service sector, rather than in traditional goods-producing industries like manufacturing or agriculture. In service economies, services are the primary drivers of economic growth and value creation.

Service Provider: A service provider is an individual, business, or organization that offers and delivers services to customers or clients. Service providers may range from independent professionals such as consultants or freelancers to large corporations providing a wide range of services.

Service Quality: Service quality refers to the level of excellence or satisfaction experienced by customers when receiving a service. It encompasses factors such as reliability, responsiveness, assurance, empathy, tangibles, and customer expectations. Ensuring high service quality is essential for customer satisfaction and loyalty.

Service Delivery: Service delivery refers to the process of providing and fulfilling services to customers or clients. It involves all the activities, interactions, and mechanisms employed to deliver the service, including communication, personnel, infrastructure, technology, and processes.

Customer Service: Customer service relates to the support and assistance provided to customers before, during, and after the purchase or use of a product or service. It focuses on addressing customer needs, inquiries, complaints, and ensuring a positive customer experience.

Service Design: Service design is a multidisciplinary approach that aims to create and improve services by considering the entire service experience. It involves understanding customer needs, designing service processes, optimizing interactions, and incorporating elements such as user experience, technology, and aesthetics.

Dependency of manufacturing on services

Manufacturing and services are interdependent sectors, and their relationship has evolved over time. Here are some key points highlighting the dependency of manufacturing on services:

1. Supply Chain and Logistics: Services play a crucial role in supporting the supply chain and logistics operations of the manufacturing sector. Transportation, warehousing, and distribution services are essential for the movement of

raw materials, components, and finished goods. Services also include inventory management, order fulfillment, and procurement, which are critical for manufacturing operations.

2. Research and Development (R&D): Services contribute significantly to the R&D efforts of the manufacturing sector. Many manufacturing companies rely on specialized research and engineering services provided by external firms to develop new products, improve processes, and enhance technological capabilities.

3. Design and Engineering: Services in design and engineering are vital for manufacturing industries. Industrial design firms, engineering consultancies, and product development services assist in conceptualizing, designing, and prototyping new products. These services contribute to innovation, efficiency, and product quality in manufacturing.

4. Technical Support and Maintenance: Manufacturing often requires technical support and maintenance services. Service providers offer installation, troubleshooting, repair, and maintenance services for machinery, equipment, and systems used in manufacturing processes. These services ensure the smooth operation and longevity of manufacturing facilities.

5. Information Technology (IT) Services: IT services are critical for modern manufacturing operations. Services such as software development, network management, cybersecurity, and data analytics support various aspects of manufacturing, including production planning, inventory control, quality management, and automation. IT services enhance efficiency, connectivity, and data-driven decision-

making in manufacturing.

6. Marketing and Sales: Services in marketing and sales are crucial for manufacturing companies to promote their products and reach customers. Advertising agencies, market research firms, and sales consulting services provide expertise in market analysis, branding, advertising campaigns, sales strategies, and customer relationship management. These services help manufacturers effectively position and sell their products in the market.

7. Training and Skills Development: Services play a significant role in providing training and skills development programs for the manufacturing workforce. Technical and vocational training providers, along with professional development services, equip manufacturing employees with the necessary knowledge and skills to operate machinery, implement best practices, and adapt to technological advancements.

8. After-Sales Service: Manufacturing companies often rely on after-sales services to provide customer support and warranty services. These services include maintenance, repairs, spare parts, and customer assistance, ensuring customer satisfaction and loyalty. After-sales services contribute to the reputation and competitiveness of manufacturers.

Economic evolution

The economic evolution of the service sector has been a significant aspect of economic development in many countries. Here is a general overview of the economic evolution of the service sector:

1. Agrarian and Industrial Economy: In traditional agrarian economies, the service sector was relatively

small, with the majority of the population engaged in agriculture. As industrialization took hold, manufacturing and goods-producing industries became dominant, leading to the growth of the industrial economy. Services during this period primarily revolved around basic necessities such as transportation, banking, and trade.

2. Post-World War II: After World War II, there was a shift in many advanced economies towards a service-oriented economy. This transition was driven by factors such as increased productivity in agriculture and manufacturing, technological advancements, and changing consumer demands. The service sector started expanding rapidly, fueled by the growth of sectors such as finance, insurance, healthcare, education, and professional services.

3. Rise of Information Technology: The advent of information technology and digitalization has been a major driver of the evolution of the service sector. The development of computer technology, the internet, and telecommunications networks has transformed the way services are delivered, creating new opportunities and enabling the globalization of services. This has led to the rise of sectors such as information technology services, e-commerce, digital media, and telecommunications.

4. Knowledge-based Economy: The service sector has increasingly shifted towards knowledge-intensive activities and intellectual capital. The knowledge-based economy is characterized by the growing importance of services that rely on specialized skills, expertise, and innovation. Professional services, research and development, software development, consulting, and creative industries have gained prominence, contributing to economic growth and

productivity.

5. Transformation and Diversification: The service sector continues to evolve and diversify, encompassing a wide range of industries and activities. New service sectors have emerged, including renewable energy, environmental services, cybersecurity, data analytics, and personalized healthcare. Services have also expanded to include experiences, entertainment, and lifestyle-oriented offerings, catering to changing consumer preferences.

6. Global Services and Offshoring: Globalization has had a significant impact on the service sector. Companies have increasingly engaged in offshoring or outsourcing services to lower-cost regions, leading to the growth of global services trade. This has facilitated the expansion of services in developing countries and created new opportunities for specialization, job creation, and economic growth.

7. Service Innovation and Entrepreneurship: Innovation and entrepreneurship have played a vital role in the economic evolution of the service sector. Service innovation involves developing new service offerings, business models, and service delivery methods to meet evolving customer needs and preferences. The rise of startups and the gig economy has also contributed to the dynamism and growth of the service sector.

8. Service-Led Economies: In many advanced economies, the service sector has become the primary driver of economic growth, employment, and value creation. Service-led economies have seen a shift away from traditional manufacturing and

heavy industries. Services contribute significantly to GDP and play a crucial role in fostering innovation, productivity, and competitiveness.

Nature of Service Sector

The service sector is characterized by several key features that distinguish it from other sectors of the economy. Here are some key aspects that define the nature of the service sector:

1. Intangibility: Services are intangible in nature, meaning they cannot be touched or physically possessed. Unlike goods, which are tangible products, services are performed or experienced. For example, receiving healthcare, consulting with a lawyer, or enjoying a live performance are all examples of services that involve intangible experiences or activities.

2. Heterogeneity: Services are often highly variable and heterogeneous due to their reliance on human interactions and personalized experiences. Each service encounter can be unique, influenced by factors such as individual preferences, skills of service providers, and specific circumstances. This heterogeneity poses challenges in standardizing and ensuring consistent service quality.

3. Perishability: Services are generally perishable and cannot be stored or inventoried. They are typically consumed or experienced at the same time they are produced. This perishability means that service providers need to manage capacity effectively to meet fluctuating demand and optimize resource utilization.

4. Simultaneity: Services are often produced and consumed simultaneously. Unlike manufacturing, where production can be separated from

consumption, services are created and delivered in real-time during the customer interaction. This characteristic can make service delivery more interactive and immediate.

5. Customer Involvement: Customers often play an active role in the production and delivery of services. They may provide information, preferences, or participate in the service process. The level of customer involvement can vary across different services, ranging from self-service models to high-touch personalized interactions.

6. Relationship and Trust: Services often involve building relationships and trust between service providers and customers. This is particularly true in industries such as healthcare, financial services, and consulting. Trust is crucial for customers to feel confident in the expertise and reliability of service providers, influencing their satisfaction and loyalty.

7. Knowledge and Expertise: Services frequently rely on specialized knowledge, skills, and expertise. Service providers, such as professionals, consultants, or technicians, possess specific knowledge and qualifications that enable them to deliver services effectively. This knowledge-based aspect differentiates many service sectors and contributes to their value.

8. Customization and Personalization: Services can be tailored to individual customer needs and preferences. Personalization allows service providers to adapt and customize offerings to meet specific customer requirements, resulting in a more personalized experience. This customization can enhance customer satisfaction and create a competitive advantage.

9. Service Delivery Networks: Service provision often involves complex networks and interactions among multiple entities. This includes coordination between service providers, suppliers, intermediaries, and customers. Effective management of these networks is crucial for ensuring smooth service delivery and customer satisfaction.

10. Emphasis on Customer Experience: The service sector places significant importance on the customer experience. Creating positive experiences, addressing customer needs, and exceeding expectations are key objectives for service providers. Delivering exceptional customer experiences can lead to customer loyalty, positive word-of-mouth, and competitive advantage.

The nature of services:

The nature of services encompasses several key characteristics that distinguish them from tangible goods. Here are the primary aspects that define the nature of services:

1. Intangibility: Services are intangible in nature, meaning they lack physical presence and cannot be touched or held. They are experiences or performances rather than physical products. For example, a haircut, consulting advice, or a software download are all examples of services.

2. Inseparability: Services are often produced and consumed simultaneously. The production and consumption of services occur in real-time, typically involving direct interaction between the service provider and the customer. This simultaneous production and consumption mean that customers are actively involved in the service delivery process.

3. Variability: Services are inherently variable and can exhibit a degree of inconsistency due to their reliance on human interactions and subjective experiences. Factors such as individual service provider skills, customer preferences, and specific circumstances can result in variations in service quality from one interaction to another.

4. Perishability: Services are perishable and cannot be stored or inventoried. They are time-sensitive and must be consumed when they are produced. The perishability of services creates challenges for service providers in managing capacity and balancing supply and demand.

5. Heterogeneity: Services are often characterized by heterogeneity or uniqueness. Each service encounter can vary depending on the specific customer, the service provider, and the context in which the service is delivered. This heterogeneity poses challenges in standardizing and ensuring consistent service quality.

6. Customer Involvement: Customers are often actively involved in the service delivery process. They may need to provide information, participate in decision-making, or contribute to the service production. The level of customer involvement can vary across different services, ranging from self-service models to highly interactive and collaborative experiences.

7. Relationship Building: Services often require the establishment of relationships and trust between service providers and customers. Building strong relationships is crucial for customer satisfaction, loyalty, and repeat business. Service providers need to understand and respond to individual customer needs to cultivate long-term relationships.

8. Knowledge and Expertise: Services often rely on specialized knowledge, skills, and expertise. Service providers, such as professionals, consultants, or technicians, possess specific expertise that enables them to deliver services effectively. The knowledge-based aspect of services adds value and differentiation to service offerings.

9. Customization and Personalization: Services can be tailored to individual customer needs and preferences. Service providers have the flexibility to customize and personalize services to meet specific customer requirements. This customization enhances customer satisfaction and creates a more personalized experience.

10. Emphasis on Customer Experience: Services place significant emphasis on the customer experience. Providing exceptional customer experiences, exceeding expectations, and addressing customer needs are essential for service providers. A positive customer experience leads to customer satisfaction, loyalty, and positive word-of-mouth.

SERVICE CLASSIFICATION

Services can be classified based on various criteria. Here are some common classifications of services:

1. Business-to-Consumer (B2C) and Business-to-Business (B2B) Services: This classification is based on the target customer segment. B2C services are directly provided to individual consumers, such as retail, healthcare, hospitality, and entertainment services. B2B services, on the other hand, cater to businesses and organizations, including professional services, consulting, logistics, and information technology services.

2. Professional Services: This category includes services that require specialized knowledge, expertise, and professional qualifications. Examples include legal services, accounting, engineering, architecture, management consulting, and medical services.

3. Financial Services: Financial services encompass services related to banking, insurance, investment, and asset management. This includes services like retail banking, mortgage lending, insurance underwriting, investment advisory, and wealth management.

4. Healthcare Services: Healthcare services involve the provision of medical care, diagnosis, treatment, and prevention of diseases. This includes services provided by hospitals, clinics, doctors, nurses, therapists, and other healthcare professionals.

5. Hospitality and Tourism Services: These services are focused on providing accommodations, food and beverage, travel, and leisure experiences. This includes hotels, restaurants, travel agencies, tour operators, theme parks, and other tourism-related services.

6. Transportation and Logistics Services: Services related to the movement of goods, people, and cargo fall under transportation and logistics. This includes services like shipping, air transport, road transport, rail transport, warehousing, freight forwarding, and supply chain management.

7. Information Technology (IT) and Telecommunications Services: This category covers services related to technology, software development, IT consulting, network management, telecommunications, and internet service providers.

8. Education and Training Services: Education services encompass various levels of learning, including primary, secondary, higher education, vocational training, and professional development programs. This also includes tutoring services, e-learning platforms, and corporate training providers.

9. Entertainment and Media Services: Services in the entertainment and media industry include film, television, music, publishing, advertising, broadcasting, gaming, and digital media platforms.

10. Personal Services: Personal services focus on meeting individual needs or providing assistance to individuals. This can include services like personal grooming, fitness and wellness, home cleaning, childcare, and elderly care.

THE SERVICE PACKAGE

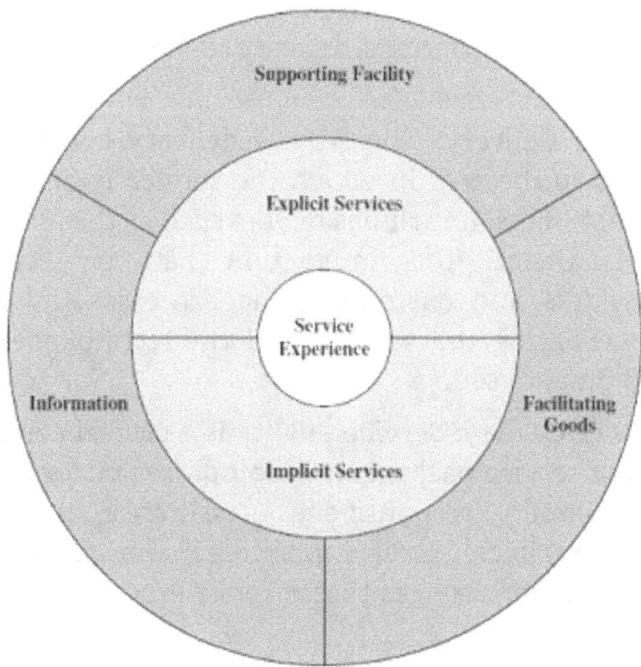

The service package refers to the combination of elements that make up a particular service offering. It encompasses all the components and features that are included when a service is delivered to customers. The service package is designed to meet customer needs, provide value, and differentiate the service from competitors. Here are some key elements typically included in a service package:

1. Core Service: The core service represents the main benefit or value that the customer receives from using the service. It is the primary reason why customers seek out the service. For example, in a hotel, the core service is providing accommodation for guests.

2. Supplementary Services: Supplementary services are additional elements that support and enhance the core service. These services may vary depending on the specific service industry and can include things like customer assistance, after-sales support, customization options, delivery services, and service guarantees.

3. Service Delivery: The service delivery component refers to the way in which the service is delivered to customers. It includes factors such as the physical environment, the interaction between service providers and customers, the processes involved in delivering the service, and the technologies or equipment used.

4. Service Quality: Service quality is a crucial element of the service package. It encompasses factors such as reliability, responsiveness, assurance, empathy, and tangibles. Service providers aim to deliver high-quality services that meet or exceed customer expectations.

5. Pricing and Payment: The pricing and payment

structure is an essential part of the service package. It includes details about the pricing model, payment methods accepted, any discounts or promotions offered, and the overall value proposition in terms of price compared to competitors.

6. Branding and Image: The service package also includes the branding and image associated with the service. This encompasses the service provider's reputation, brand identity, and the perception that customers have of the service. Branding and image influence customer trust, loyalty, and the overall perception of the service.

7. Service Access: Service access refers to how customers can access and utilize the service. It includes aspects such as availability, convenience, reservation systems, booking processes, and any limitations or restrictions that may apply.

8. Customer Support: Customer support is an integral part of the service package, providing assistance to customers before, during, and after the service delivery. It includes customer service channels, such as phone, email, or chat support, as well as self-service options, FAQs, and online resources.

9. Service Guarantees: Service guarantees are assurances provided by the service provider to customers regarding the quality, performance, or specific outcomes of the service. They help build customer confidence and trust in the service.

10. Service Innovation: The service package should also reflect ongoing efforts to innovate and improve the service offering. This can include introducing new features, technologies, or service enhancements based on customer feedback, market trends, or industry advancements.

CHARACTERISTICS OF SERVICE OPERATIONS

Service operations possess distinct characteristics that differentiate them from manufacturing or goods-based operations. Understanding these characteristics is crucial for managing and delivering services effectively. Here are the key characteristics of service operations:

1. Intangibility: Services are intangible, meaning they lack physical form and cannot be touched or held. Unlike tangible goods, services are experienced and consumed rather than owned. This characteristic poses challenges in terms of marketing, evaluation, and quality assurance as customers cannot physically examine or assess services before consumption.

2. Simultaneity: Service production and consumption often occur simultaneously, with customers actively involved in the process. Service providers interact directly with customers, resulting in real-time service delivery. This characteristic necessitates effective coordination and synchronization between service providers and customers to ensure a smooth and satisfactory experience.

3. Perishability: Services are typically perishable and cannot be stored or inventoried. They must be consumed at the time of production, and any unused capacity is lost. The perishability of services requires careful management of capacity and demand to optimize resource utilization and minimize service gaps.

4. Variability: Services exhibit variability due to their reliance on human interactions, customer preferences, and situational factors. Each service encounter can differ in terms of the performance,

quality, and customer experience. Managing and maintaining consistent service quality can be challenging due to this inherent variability.

5. Customer Participation: Customers often play an active role in service delivery, requiring their participation throughout the service process. Customers may provide information, make decisions, and contribute to the outcome of the service. This characteristic necessitates effective communication, collaboration, and customization to meet individual customer needs and preferences.

6. Relationship Orientation: Services are often based on building and nurturing relationships between service providers and customers. Establishing trust, understanding customer preferences, and delivering personalized experiences are crucial for creating and maintaining long-term customer relationships. Relationship building is a key aspect of service operations.

7. Knowledge and Expertise: Services often rely on specialized knowledge, skills, and expertise. Service providers must possess the necessary qualifications and expertise to deliver services effectively. This characteristic emphasizes the importance of training, continuous learning, and professional development within service operations.

8. Service Environment: The service environment, including physical settings and atmosphere, can significantly influence the customer experience. Creating a pleasant and conducive environment is vital for enhancing customer satisfaction and perception of service quality. Service operations must consider the design and management of the service environment.

9. Time Sensitivity: Time is a critical factor in service operations. Customers often expect prompt and timely service delivery. Managing wait times, response times, and service duration is essential to meet customer expectations and minimize customer dissatisfaction.

10. Service Quality and Customer Satisfaction: Service quality and customer satisfaction are of paramount importance in service operations. Meeting or exceeding customer expectations and delivering high-quality service experiences are vital for customer loyalty and positive word-of-mouth. Service operations must prioritize continuous improvement and customer-centric approaches.

CLASSIFYING SERVICES FOR STRATEGIC INSIGHTS

Classifying services can provide strategic insights and help organizations better understand their service offerings, target markets, and competitive advantages. Here are several common approaches to classifying services for strategic insights:

1. Service Characteristics: Classifying services based on their characteristics helps identify commonalities and differences among services, allowing organizations to tailor their strategies accordingly. Examples of characteristics include intangibility, perishability, customer involvement, and level of customization.

2. Service Process: Analyzing the service process can provide insights into the operational aspects of service delivery. Services can be classified based on the degree of customer contact, customer participation, complexity, and the level of standardization or customization involved in the process.

3. Service Industry or Sector: Grouping services based on industry or sector helps organizations understand industry-specific dynamics, competition, and trends. Industries such as healthcare, finance, hospitality, transportation, information technology, and professional services each have their own unique characteristics and strategic considerations.

4. Service Value Chain: Examining the service value chain can provide insights into the different stages involved in creating and delivering the service. This classification may include activities such as service design, marketing and sales, service delivery, customer support, and after-sales service. Understanding the value chain can identify areas for improvement, cost optimization, and differentiation.

5. Service Target Market: Classifying services based on the target market helps organizations tailor their marketing strategies and identify specific customer needs and preferences. This can include consumer services, business services, government services, or services targeting specific demographic segments or industries.

6. Service Lifecycle: Services can be classified based on their lifecycle stages, such as introduction, growth, maturity, and decline. Understanding where a service stands in its lifecycle can inform strategic decisions regarding investment, marketing, innovation, and resource allocation.

7. Service Innovativeness: Classifying services based on their level of innovativeness provides insights into the organization's innovation capabilities and potential competitive advantages. Services can

range from incremental improvements to radical innovations, and understanding the level of innovation helps organizations focus their efforts and resources accordingly.

8. Service Pricing and Positioning: Analyzing the pricing and positioning of services can provide strategic insights into market positioning, value proposition, and differentiation. Services can be classified based on pricing strategies, such as premium services, value-for-money offerings, or low-cost alternatives.

9. Service Ecosystem: Examining the broader ecosystem in which a service operates helps organizations understand the interdependencies, partnerships, and value networks involved. This classification can include analyzing the relationships between service providers, customers, suppliers, and other stakeholders within the ecosystem.

10. Service Delivery Channels: Classifying services based on the delivery channels employed, such as physical locations, online platforms, mobile apps, or self-service kiosks, provides insights into customer touchpoints, convenience, and the integration of technology.

SYSTEMS VIEW OF SERVICES

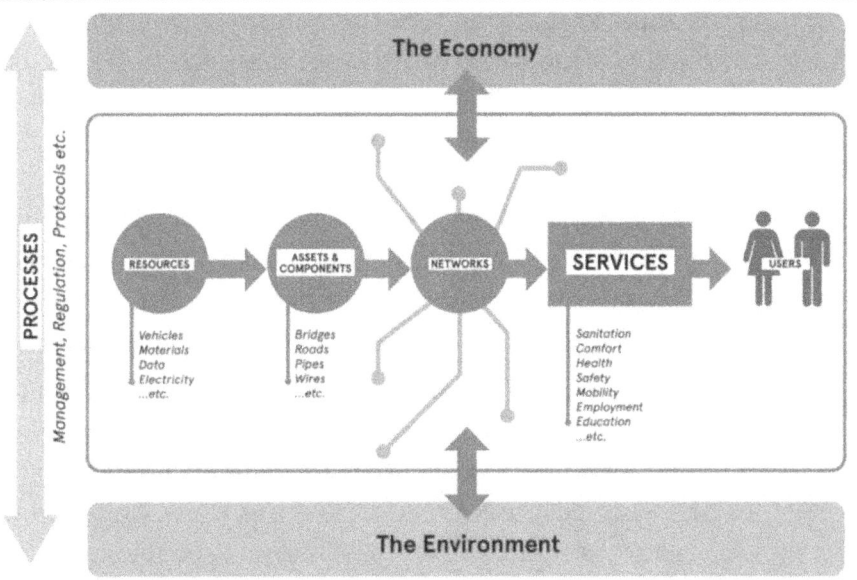

The systems view of services recognizes that services are not isolated entities but rather complex systems with various interrelated components and interactions. It focuses on understanding and managing the interdependencies and relationships between different elements within the service system. Here are key aspects of the systems view of services:

1. Service System Components: A service system consists of multiple components, including customers, service providers, technology, processes, infrastructure, resources, and supporting organizations. These components interact and collaborate to create and deliver the service.

2. Interactions and Relationships: The systems view emphasizes the interactions and relationships between different components within the service system. It recognizes that the quality of these interactions directly affects the overall service experience and value delivered to customers. Effective management of these relationships is crucial for optimizing service performance.

3. Feedback Loops: The systems view considers feedback loops within the service system. Feedback loops capture information about customer needs, preferences, and satisfaction, which is used to continuously improve service quality and performance. Feedback loops enable organizations to monitor, evaluate, and adapt their service offerings based on customer feedback.

4. Value Co-Creation: Services are co-created through the collaboration and interaction between service providers and customers. The systems view acknowledges that customers play an active role in the service process, contributing their knowledge, resources, and inputs. Service providers and customers jointly create value, and the systems perspective emphasizes the importance of customer engagement and involvement.

5. System Boundaries: The systems view recognizes that service systems have boundaries that define their scope and interactions. These boundaries determine which components and entities are included within the service system and which are external to it. Understanding system boundaries is essential for managing dependencies and interactions effectively.

6. Service Ecosystems: Services exist within broader ecosystems, consisting of interconnected entities, such as suppliers, partners, competitors, regulatory bodies, and complementary service providers. The systems view acknowledges the interdependencies and relationships within the service ecosystem and the impact of external factors on service performance.

7. System Dynamics: The systems view considers

the dynamic nature of service systems. Service systems are subject to changes, disruptions, and evolving customer needs. The systems perspective helps organizations understand and anticipate these dynamics, enabling them to proactively adapt their strategies and operations.

8. Performance Metrics: The systems view emphasizes the need for holistic performance metrics that capture the overall effectiveness and efficiency of the service system. These metrics go beyond traditional measures and consider factors such as customer satisfaction, service quality, resource utilization, process efficiency, and value creation.

9. Continuous Improvement: The systems view promotes a culture of continuous improvement within the service system. It recognizes that service systems are not static but evolve over time. Organizations strive to identify opportunities for innovation, efficiency gains, and service enhancements through ongoing evaluation, learning, and adaptation.

10. Service System Resilience: The systems view acknowledges the importance of building resilience within service systems. Resilience enables service systems to respond and recover effectively from disruptions, changes in demand, or unforeseen events. It involves the ability to adapt, maintain service continuity, and ensure customer satisfaction even in challenging circumstances.

SERVICE STRATEGY:

Service strategy refers to the deliberate and planned approach that organizations adopt to deliver value and achieve their service-related objectives. It involves making strategic decisions and setting directions for service offerings, customer experiences, resource allocation, and competitive positioning. Here are key elements and considerations in developing a service strategy:

1. Value Proposition: Define the unique value that your services offer to customers. This involves understanding customer needs, preferences, and pain points, and aligning your service offerings to address them effectively. Your value proposition should clearly communicate the benefits, outcomes, and differentiation that customers can expect from your services.

2. Target Market Segmentation: Identify and segment your target market based on relevant characteristics, such as demographics, psychographics, behaviors, or industry. This enables you to tailor your service offerings, marketing strategies, and customer experiences to specific customer segments that have distinct needs and preferences.

3. Service Differentiation: Determine how your services will stand out from competitors. This can be achieved through various means, such as offering unique features, superior quality, personalized experiences, exceptional customer service, innovative approaches, or specialized expertise. Service differentiation helps create a competitive advantage and attract target customers.

4. Service Delivery Model: Define the service delivery model that aligns with your target market and business objectives. This includes decisions on delivery channels (e.g., physical locations, online platforms, mobile apps), customer touchpoints,

service processes, technology utilization, and integration of self-service options. The chosen service delivery model should optimize customer convenience, efficiency, and value creation.

5. Service Design and Innovation: Focus on designing services that are customer-centric and align with their evolving needs. Apply design thinking principles to understand customer journeys, pain points, and opportunities for service improvement. Foster a culture of service innovation, encouraging employees to generate and implement ideas for new services, service enhancements, and process improvements.

6. Service Quality and Standards: Establish service quality standards and define metrics to measure and monitor service performance. Develop processes and systems to ensure consistent service delivery, address customer feedback, and continuously improve service quality. Consider implementing service certifications or quality management frameworks to reinforce a commitment to service excellence.

7. Service Pricing and Revenue Models: Determine the pricing strategy and revenue models that align with your value proposition, cost structure, and customer willingness to pay. Consider factors such as cost-based pricing, value-based pricing, competitive pricing, subscription models, tiered pricing, or bundled offerings. Pricing decisions should support your overall service strategy and revenue goals.

8. Customer Experience Management: Develop a comprehensive customer experience strategy that encompasses all touchpoints and interactions with customers. Design seamless and personalized

experiences that align with your brand promise and customer expectations. Implement customer feedback mechanisms, measure customer satisfaction, and continuously refine the customer experience based on insights.

9. Service Partnerships and Alliances: Explore partnerships and alliances that can enhance your service offerings, extend your reach, or provide access to complementary capabilities or resources. Collaborations with other organizations can help expand service capabilities, improve competitiveness, and tap into new market opportunities.

10. Monitoring and Adaptation: Continuously monitor market trends, customer preferences, and competitive landscape to stay informed and responsive. Regularly review and assess the effectiveness of your service strategy, making adjustments as needed to remain aligned with market dynamics and organizational goals.

STRATEGIC SERVICE VISION

A strategic service vision is a forward-looking statement that outlines the desired future state and direction for the organization's service offerings. It provides a clear and compelling image of the organization's aspirations, purpose, and strategic goals related to services. Here are key elements and considerations in developing a strategic service vision:

1. Future State: Describe the envisioned future state for the organization's services. This includes articulating the desired outcomes, impact, and value that the organization aims to deliver to its customers and stakeholders. The future state should align with the organization's overall mission, vision, and

strategic objectives.

2. Customer-Centric Focus: Emphasize a customer-centric approach in the strategic service vision. Clearly articulate how the organization will understand and meet the evolving needs, expectations, and preferences of its target customers. Highlight the organization's commitment to delivering exceptional customer experiences and creating customer value.

3. Differentiation and Competitive Advantage: Identify how the organization's services will differentiate from competitors and create a sustainable competitive advantage. Highlight unique features, capabilities, or approaches that set the organization apart and make its services distinct and valuable in the marketplace.

4. Innovation and Adaptability: Emphasize the importance of innovation and adaptability in the strategic service vision. Communicate the organization's commitment to continuously improving services, embracing new technologies, and adapting to changing customer demands, market dynamics, and industry trends.

5. Service Excellence and Quality: Promote a culture of service excellence and a commitment to delivering high-quality services. Clearly state the organization's expectations for service quality, performance standards, and continuous improvement efforts. Demonstrate the organization's dedication to achieving and maintaining service excellence.

6. Organizational Alignment: Ensure the strategic service vision aligns with the overall organizational strategy and goals. It should be consistent with the organization's mission, vision, values, and

strategic priorities. Communicate how the strategic service vision supports the broader organizational objectives and contributes to its long-term success.

7. Employee Engagement and Empowerment: Engage employees in the strategic service vision by emphasizing their role in delivering exceptional service experiences. Demonstrate how the organization will empower and support employees to provide superior service, develop their skills, and contribute to the achievement of the strategic service vision.

8. Measurable Objectives: Set measurable objectives and key performance indicators (KPIs) that will be used to track progress and evaluate the success of the strategic service vision. Define specific goals related to customer satisfaction, service quality, market share, revenue growth, or other relevant metrics.

9. Communication and Commitment: Clearly communicate the strategic service vision throughout the organization, ensuring it is well understood and embraced at all levels. Encourage employee commitment and alignment with the vision. Develop communication plans to regularly reinforce the vision and provide updates on progress.

10. Continuous Evaluation and Refinement: Recognize that the strategic service vision may need to evolve over time. Establish mechanisms for continuous evaluation, feedback, and refinement of the vision to ensure its relevance and effectiveness. Regularly review and assess the organization's progress towards achieving the strategic service vision.

COMPETITIVE SERVICE STRATEGIES

Competitive service strategies are approaches that

organizations adopt to gain a competitive advantage in the marketplace and differentiate their service offerings from competitors. These strategies aim to attract and retain customers, increase market share, and achieve long-term success. Here are some key competitive service strategies:

1. Differentiation Strategy: Focus on creating unique and distinctive service offerings that stand out in the market. Differentiation can be achieved through innovative features, customization options, superior service quality, personalized experiences, or specialized expertise. The goal is to provide customers with a compelling reason to choose your services over competitors.

2. Cost Leadership Strategy: Emphasize cost efficiency and competitive pricing to offer services at lower prices than competitors. This strategy requires optimizing operational processes, streamlining resource utilization, and leveraging economies of scale. By offering affordable services, organizations can attract price-sensitive customers and gain a competitive edge.

3. Focus Strategy: Concentrate on serving a specific market segment or niche with specialized services. This strategy involves deeply understanding the needs, preferences, and unique characteristics of the target market and tailoring services to meet their specific requirements. By focusing on a particular customer segment, organizations can deliver highly relevant and differentiated services.

4. Innovation Strategy: Prioritize continuous innovation and the development of new service offerings. This can involve introducing new features, leveraging emerging technologies, adopting new service delivery models, or creating entirely new

services. By being at the forefront of innovation, organizations can differentiate themselves and stay ahead of competitors.

5. Service Excellence Strategy: Establish a strong reputation for delivering exceptional service experiences. This strategy focuses on providing outstanding customer service, exceeding customer expectations, and consistently delivering high-quality services. Organizations can achieve service excellence through employee training, service standards, customer feedback mechanisms, and a customer-centric culture.

6. Partnerships and Alliances Strategy: Form strategic partnerships or alliances with other organizations to enhance service offerings or expand market reach. Collaborations can involve complementary service providers, technology providers, suppliers, or industry associations. By leveraging the capabilities and resources of partners, organizations can enhance their service portfolio and provide comprehensive solutions to customers.

7. Customer Relationship Strategy: Build strong, long-term relationships with customers by fostering customer loyalty and engagement. This strategy involves understanding individual customer needs, preferences, and behaviors, and tailoring service interactions accordingly. It includes personalized communication, proactive customer support, loyalty programs, and customer feedback mechanisms to continuously improve service delivery.

8. Branding and Reputation Strategy: Develop a strong brand image and reputation associated with quality, reliability, and trustworthiness. This

strategy focuses on building a positive brand perception through effective marketing, consistent service delivery, positive customer experiences, and leveraging customer testimonials and reviews. A strong brand can attract and retain customers, even in highly competitive markets.

9. Service Convenience Strategy: Emphasize convenience and ease of access in service delivery. This strategy involves offering multiple service channels, such as online platforms, mobile apps, self-service options, and extended operating hours. By providing convenient and accessible services, organizations can enhance the customer experience and gain a competitive advantage.

10. Continuous Improvement Strategy: Foster a culture of continuous improvement within the organization. This strategy focuses on constantly assessing and enhancing service quality, operational efficiency, and customer satisfaction. It involves gathering customer feedback, monitoring market trends, benchmarking against competitors, and implementing process improvements to stay ahead in the competitive landscape.

WINNING CUSTOMERS IN MARKETPLACE

Winning customers in the marketplace requires a strategic approach that focuses on understanding customer needs, delivering value, and differentiating your offerings from competitors. Here are some key strategies for winning customers:

1. Market Research and Segmentation: Conduct thorough market research to understand your target customers, their demographics, preferences, and pain points. Segment your target market based on

relevant characteristics and tailor your marketing efforts to each segment's specific needs and preferences.

2. Value Proposition: Clearly define and communicate your unique value proposition. Identify the key benefits and value that your offerings provide to customers and articulate them in a compelling way. Differentiate your offerings by highlighting what sets them apart and how they address customer needs better than competitors.

3. Customer Experience: Focus on providing exceptional customer experiences at every touchpoint. Prioritize responsiveness, personalized interactions, convenience, and consistent service quality. Invest in training your employees to deliver outstanding customer service and create positive, memorable interactions.

4. Product/Service Quality: Ensure that your products or services meet or exceed customer expectations in terms of quality, reliability, and performance. Continuous improvement efforts should be in place to address any issues, enhance features, and stay ahead of evolving customer needs.

5. Competitive Pricing: Set competitive pricing that provides value to customers while still maintaining profitability. Conduct pricing analysis to ensure your pricing aligns with customer perceptions and market trends. Consider pricing strategies such as cost leadership, premium pricing, or value-based pricing, depending on your market positioning and customer segment.

6. Effective Marketing and Promotion: Develop a comprehensive marketing and promotion strategy to reach and engage your target customers. Utilize a

mix of channels, including digital marketing, social media, content marketing, advertising, and public relations. Craft persuasive messages that resonate with your audience and communicate the benefits of your offerings effectively.

7. Customer Relationship Building: Build strong relationships with customers by fostering trust, providing ongoing support, and staying engaged. Implement customer relationship management (CRM) systems to track customer interactions, preferences, and feedback. Use this information to personalize your communications and offerings, and provide proactive support.

8. Referral Programs and Customer Advocacy: Encourage satisfied customers to refer your products or services to others. Implement referral programs or incentivize customer advocacy to reward customers for recommending your offerings. Positive word-of-mouth can be a powerful driver for acquiring new customers.

9. Differentiation and Innovation: Continuously innovate and differentiate your offerings to stay ahead of the competition. Identify customer pain points, market trends, and emerging technologies to develop new features, services, or approaches that provide added value to customers. Highlight these innovations as part of your value proposition.

10. Monitoring and Adaptation: Regularly monitor customer feedback, market trends, and competitor activities to adapt your strategies and offerings accordingly. Stay responsive to changing customer needs and preferences, and continuously refine your marketing and service delivery to maintain a competitive edge.

STAGES IN SERVICE FIRM COMPETITIVENESS

The competitiveness of a service firm evolves through various stages as it develops and adapts to the market dynamics and customer needs. Here are the general stages in service firm competitiveness:

1. Initiation: The initiation stage marks the beginning of a service firm's operations. It involves setting up the business, defining the value proposition, and establishing a presence in the market. At this stage, the firm focuses on building its foundational capabilities, such as assembling a team, developing basic processes, and acquiring initial customers.

2. Survival: In the survival stage, the service firm aims to establish its viability and sustainability. The focus is on generating sufficient revenue to cover costs and achieve profitability. The firm may face challenges in attracting customers, gaining market share, and establishing a strong reputation. Strategic decisions are made to overcome initial obstacles and create a stable foundation for growth.

3. Growth: During the growth stage, the service firm experiences an expansion in its customer base, revenue, and market presence. Investments are made to scale operations, enhance service offerings, and improve efficiencies. The focus shifts towards capturing a larger market share, expanding geographically, and increasing the range of services provided. This stage requires effective resource management, strong customer acquisition strategies, and operational scalability.

4. Differentiation: As the service firm grows, it enters the differentiation stage, where it seeks to distinguish itself from competitors and create

a unique market position. The firm focuses on developing specialized capabilities, innovating service offerings, and delivering exceptional customer experiences. Differentiation strategies may involve leveraging technology, personalization, customization, or industry-specific expertise to provide a competitive advantage.

5. Leadership: The leadership stage represents the firm's position as a market leader or a significant player within its industry. The firm has achieved substantial market share, brand recognition, and customer loyalty. The focus shifts towards maintaining and extending market leadership through continuous innovation, strategic partnerships, and superior customer value delivery. The firm is seen as a benchmark for competitors and shapes industry trends.

6. Adaptation and Renewal: Over time, the competitive landscape and customer preferences change. In the adaptation and renewal stage, the service firm continuously monitors the market and adapts its strategies, offerings, and operations to remain relevant and competitive. This stage involves a proactive approach to anticipate market shifts, embrace new technologies, and adopt agile practices. The firm emphasizes continuous learning, innovation, and customer-centricity to sustain its competitiveness.

MEASURING SERVICE PRODUCTIVITY

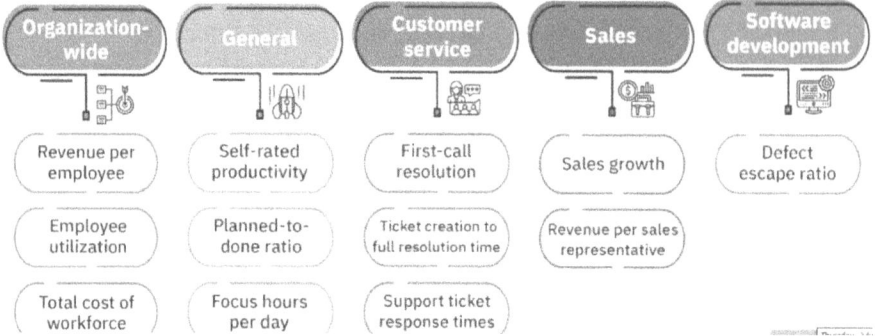

Measuring service productivity can be challenging due to the intangible nature of services and the variety of factors that contribute to service delivery. However, several approaches and metrics can be used to assess service productivity. Here are some common methods:

1. Output-Based Measures: These measures focus on quantifying the output or outcomes generated by the service. For example:

    · Number of customers served: This metric tracks the volume of customers or clients served within a specific period.

    · Service units delivered: Measure the number of specific service units provided, such as consultations, treatments, or transactions.

    · Revenue generated: Assess the monetary value of services rendered, indicating the financial output of the service operation.

2. Input-Based Measures: These measures evaluate the resources utilized to deliver services. They help assess efficiency and resource allocation. Examples include:

- Labor hours or full-time equivalents (FTE): Measure the number of hours or FTEs required to deliver services.

- Equipment utilization: Assess the utilization rate of equipment or technology used in service delivery.

- Cost per unit of service: Calculate the cost required to deliver a specific service unit.

3. Customer-Based Measures: These measures focus on customer satisfaction and the quality of the service experience. While not directly measuring productivity, customer satisfaction is often an indicator of the effectiveness of service delivery. Examples include:

   - Customer satisfaction surveys: Collect feedback from customers on their satisfaction with the service experience.

   - Net Promoter Score (NPS): Measure the likelihood of customers recommending the service to others.

   - Customer complaints and resolution time: Track the number of customer complaints and the time taken to resolve them.

4. Efficiency Measures: These measures assess the efficiency of service operations and processes. They aim to identify bottlenecks, streamline workflows, and eliminate waste. Examples include:

   - Service cycle time: Measure the time taken to complete a service from start to finish.

   - Staff productivity ratios: Assess the ratio of output to input, such as the number of customers served per employee or revenue per employee.

- Service delivery cost ratios: Calculate the cost of service delivery relative to the revenue generated.

5. Benchmarking: Compare service productivity metrics against industry benchmarks or best practices. This allows for a broader perspective on performance and helps identify areas for improvement.

CHAPTER 2

DESIGNING THE SERVICE ENTERPRISE:

Designing a service enterprise involves strategically planning and creating the framework for delivering high-quality services that meet customer needs and drive business success. Here are key steps to consider when designing a service enterprise:

1. Define the Service Vision and Objectives: Clearly articulate the purpose, vision, and objectives of the service enterprise. This includes identifying the target market, understanding customer needs, and establishing the desired outcomes and value proposition that the enterprise aims to deliver.

2. Conduct Market Research and Analysis: Gain a deep understanding of the market landscape, customer preferences, and industry trends. Conduct market research, analyze customer behavior, and assess competitors to identify opportunities and potential gaps in the market.

3. Service Portfolio Development: Develop a comprehensive service portfolio that aligns with the service vision and meets the needs of the target market. Consider the breadth and depth of services, differentiators, pricing strategies, and potential service bundling or packaging options.

4. Service Design and Innovation: Use design thinking principles and customer-centric approaches to design services that deliver exceptional customer

experiences. Focus on understanding customer journeys, pain points, and preferences, and integrate these insights into service design and innovation efforts.

5. Process and Operational Design: Design efficient and effective processes and operations that support service delivery. Identify key process steps, roles and responsibilities, workflows, and technology requirements. Pay attention to service flow, customer touchpoints, and ways to streamline operations for better efficiency and resource utilization.

6. Service Culture and Employee Engagement: Cultivate a service-oriented culture within the enterprise. Foster a customer-centric mindset among employees and provide training and development opportunities to enhance their service skills. Encourage employee engagement and empowerment, as they play a crucial role in delivering exceptional service experiences.

7. Technology and Infrastructure: Determine the technology and infrastructure needed to support service delivery. Assess the requirements for customer interactions, data management, service tracking, and operational efficiency. Implement appropriate technologies, such as customer relationship management (CRM) systems, service automation tools, or data analytics platforms, to enhance service capabilities.

8. Service Quality Assurance: Develop mechanisms to ensure and monitor service quality. Establish service standards, implement quality control processes, and define performance metrics to measure service effectiveness and customer satisfaction. Regularly

evaluate service performance and seek customer feedback to identify areas for improvement.

9. Customer Engagement and Marketing: Develop strategies to engage and attract customers. Build strong relationships through effective marketing, customer communication, and personalized experiences. Utilize various marketing channels, including digital platforms, social media, content marketing, and referral programs, to promote the service enterprise and create brand awareness.

10. Continuous Improvement and Adaptation: Embrace a culture of continuous improvement and adaptation. Regularly evaluate the effectiveness of the service enterprise, monitor market dynamics, and stay informed about customer needs and preferences. Make necessary adjustments, innovate service offerings, and proactively respond to changing market conditions to ensure the enterprise remains competitive.

NEW SERVICE DEVELOPMENT:

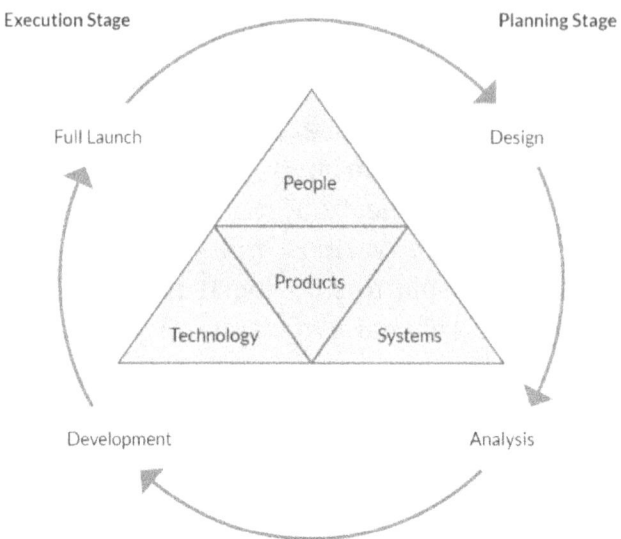

New service development refers to the process of creating and introducing innovative and unique services to the market. It involves identifying customer needs, generating ideas, designing service offerings, testing and refining concepts, and launching the new services. Here are key steps involved in the new service development process:

1. Idea Generation: Start by generating ideas for new services. This can be done through various methods, such as brainstorming sessions, customer feedback, market research, competitor analysis, or leveraging emerging technologies and trends. Encourage creativity and collaboration within the organization to generate a wide range of ideas.

2. Idea Screening: Evaluate and screen the generated ideas to identify the most promising ones. Assess the feasibility, alignment with the organization's goals and resources, market potential, and competitive advantage of each idea. Eliminate ideas that are not viable or do not fit the strategic objectives of the organization.

3. Concept Development: Develop detailed concepts for the selected ideas. Define the value proposition, target market, key features, pricing, delivery channels, and potential customer benefits. Consider the unique selling points and differentiation factors that set the new service apart from existing offerings.

4. Market Research and Analysis: Conduct thorough market research to understand the target market and customer needs. Identify the size of the market, customer segments, preferences, and pain points. Gather insights on market trends, competition, and potential demand for the new service. Use market research to validate and refine the service concept.

5. Service Design: Design the new service based on the insights gathered. Define the service process, customer journey, touchpoints, and interactions. Focus on creating a seamless and customer-centric experience that addresses the identified customer needs and pain points. Consider service blueprints, prototyping, or mock-ups to visualize and refine the service design.

6. Testing and Validation: Test the new service concept and prototype in a controlled environment or with a small group of customers. Gather feedback, evaluate the customer response, and assess the feasibility and effectiveness of the service design. Use this feedback to make necessary refinements and enhancements to the service.

7. Business Modeling: Develop a business model for the new service. Assess the revenue streams, cost structure, pricing strategy, and resource requirements. Consider financial projections, profitability, and sustainability of the new service.

Determine the investment needed and potential return on investment.

8. Implementation and Launch: Prepare for the launch of the new service. Develop a detailed implementation plan, including marketing and communication strategies, resource allocation, training, and operational readiness. Execute the plan and introduce the new service to the target market. Monitor the launch process and make adjustments as needed.

9. Evaluation and Continuous Improvement: Continuously evaluate the performance and customer response to the new service. Monitor key performance indicators, customer satisfaction, and market feedback. Gather insights to identify areas for improvement and make necessary adjustments to enhance the service. Maintain a feedback loop to incorporate customer feedback and iterate on the service design.

10. Post-Launch Monitoring: After the launch, closely monitor the performance and success of the new service. Analyze customer adoption, revenue generation, and market share. Regularly review and refine the service offering based on market dynamics, customer needs, and competitive landscape.

SERVICE DESIGN ELEMENTS

Service Design Elements

Design Elements	Topics
Structural	
Delivery system	Process structure, service blueprint, strategic positioning
Facility design	Servicescapes, architecture, process flows, layout
Location	Geographic demand, site selection, location strategy
Capacity planning	Strategic role, queuing models, planning criteria
Managerial	
Information	Technology, scalability, use of Internet
Quality	Measurement, design quality, recovery, tools, six-sigma
Service encounter	Encounter triad, culture, supply relationships, outsourcing
Managing capacity and demand	Strategies, yield management, queue management

Service design is the process of designing and improving services to meet customer needs and create positive user experiences. It involves considering various elements and factors that contribute to the overall service delivery. Here are some key elements of service design:

1. User Research: Service design begins with understanding the needs, behaviors, and preferences of the users or customers. User research techniques, such as interviews, surveys, and observations, help gather insights into user expectations, pain points, and desired outcomes.

2. Service Blueprint: A service blueprint is a visual representation of the service journey that outlines the steps involved in service delivery, including interactions, touchpoints, and backend processes. It helps identify potential gaps, inefficiencies, and

opportunities for improvement.

3. Service Environment: The physical and virtual environment in which the service is delivered greatly impacts the user experience. Service design considers factors such as interior design, layout, signage, lighting, ambiance, and digital interfaces to create an inviting and user-friendly environment.

4. Service Processes and Flows: Designing efficient and effective service processes is crucial for a seamless user experience. Service design defines the steps, roles, responsibilities, and interactions involved in delivering the service. It aims to eliminate bottlenecks, streamline workflows, and optimize resource utilization.

5. Service Touchpoints: Touchpoints are the moments of interaction between the user and the service provider. Service design considers all touchpoints, including in-person interactions, phone calls, website interfaces, mobile apps, social media, and other communication channels. Each touchpoint should be designed to be user-friendly, consistent, and aligned with the overall service experience.

6. Service Interactions: Interactions between service providers and users greatly impact the user experience. Service design focuses on training and empowering service providers to deliver exceptional customer service, handle inquiries and complaints, and create positive interactions at each customer touchpoint.

7. Service Offerings: The design of the service itself is a critical element. It involves defining the features, benefits, and value proposition of the service. Service design considers customization options, service levels, packaging, pricing, and service delivery

channels to ensure the service meets user needs and aligns with organizational objectives.

8. Service Communication: Effective communication is essential for informing users about the service, setting expectations, and providing updates. Service design considers how information is communicated through various channels, including marketing materials, websites, mobile apps, signage, and customer support interactions.

9. Service Metrics and Feedback: Service design incorporates methods for gathering user feedback and measuring service performance. This includes customer satisfaction surveys, Net Promoter Score (NPS), and other metrics to assess the user experience and identify areas for improvement.

10. Service Culture and Organization: The culture and organization of the service provider play a significant role in service delivery. Service design considers factors such as employee training, organizational structure, incentives, and values to foster a customer-centric culture that supports the delivery of exceptional services.

SERVICE BLUEPRINTING

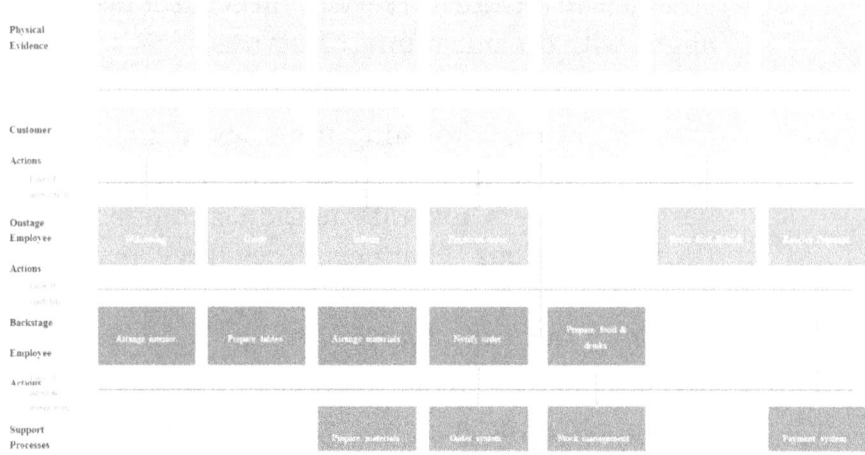

Service blueprinting is a visual representation and detailed mapping of the service process, interactions, and touchpoints involved in delivering a service. It provides a holistic view of the service journey, including the front-stage (customer-facing) and back-stage (behind-the-scenes) processes. Service blueprinting helps organizations identify pain points, bottlenecks, and opportunities for improvement in service delivery. Here are the key components and steps involved in service blueprinting:

1. Service Process: Start by identifying the key steps and activities involved in the service process. This includes both customer-visible activities and those that occur behind the scenes. Determine the sequence of these activities, including any dependencies or handoffs between different stages.

2. Front-Stage Interactions: Identify the touchpoints and interactions between the service provider and the customer. This includes any face-to-face interactions, phone calls, online interactions, or other communication channels. Note the specific actions, information exchange, and customer experiences at each touchpoint.

3. Back-Stage Processes: Determine the behind-the-scenes processes and activities that support the

service delivery. These may involve tasks such as data entry, inventory management, service preparation, or coordination between different departments. Include relevant interactions and dependencies between front-stage and back-stage processes.

4. Support Processes: Consider the support processes that enable the service delivery, such as customer support, billing, technical assistance, or quality assurance. Identify how these processes integrate with the core service process and interact with the customer or the front-stage staff.

5. Physical Evidence and Technology: Note the physical evidence or tangible elements that customers interact with during the service journey. This includes signage, equipment, facilities, or digital interfaces. Also, identify the technology infrastructure and systems used to support service delivery and streamline processes.

6. Roles and Responsibilities: Assign roles and responsibilities to each activity and touchpoint in the service blueprint. This includes identifying the personnel or departments responsible for specific tasks and interactions. Clarify the division of responsibilities between the service provider and the customer.

7. Time and Sequence: Indicate the time required for each activity, touchpoint, or process step. Show the sequence of events and interactions to visualize the flow of the service process. This helps identify any potential delays, waiting times, or inefficiencies in the service journey.

8. Pain Points and Opportunities: Analyze the service blueprint to identify pain points, bottlenecks, or

areas for improvement. Look for opportunities to enhance the customer experience, streamline processes, or eliminate unnecessary steps. Consider how technology or process changes can address pain points and optimize service delivery.

STRATEGIC POSITIONING THROUGH PROCESS STRUCTURE

Strategic Positioning through Process Structure

- ### Degree of Complexity
  - ❑ Measured by the number of steps in the service blueprint. For example, a medical clinic is less complex than a general hospital.
- ### Degree of Divergence
  - ❑ Amount of discretion permitted the server to customize the service. For example, a high-end vs. low-end hotel has more personalized services.

Strategic positioning through process structure involves designing and organizing the internal processes of an organization in a way that aligns with its strategic objectives and enhances its competitive advantage. It involves making deliberate choices about how processes are structured, coordinated, and optimized to support the organization's strategic goals. Here are key considerations for strategic positioning through process structure:

1. Aligning Processes with Strategy: Understand the organization's strategic objectives and identify the critical processes that drive value creation. Align process structure with the strategic goals by ensuring that process design, resource allocation,

and coordination support the desired outcomes. This may involve focusing on cost leadership, differentiation, customer intimacy, or innovation, depending on the strategic positioning of the organization.

2. Process Mapping and Analysis: Map and analyze existing processes to identify inefficiencies, bottlenecks, and areas for improvement. Use process mapping techniques, such as flowcharts or value stream mapping, to visualize the sequence of activities, dependencies, and handoffs within processes. This analysis helps identify opportunities to streamline processes, eliminate waste, and enhance overall efficiency.

3. Process Standardization and Simplification: Standardize and simplify processes to improve consistency, reduce complexity, and enhance scalability. Identify commonalities and best practices across different process areas and create standardized process templates or guidelines. This helps drive efficiency, reduce errors, and improve coordination across the organization.

4. Process Integration and Coordination: Foster integration and coordination among different processes to ensure smooth workflow and information flow. Break down functional silos and encourage cross-functional collaboration. Implement mechanisms for effective communication, handoffs, and feedback loops between different process areas. This integration enhances organizational agility, responsiveness, and customer-centricity.

5. Technology Enablement: Leverage technology to automate and streamline processes. Identify

opportunities for process digitization, workflow automation, data integration, and real-time monitoring. Implement appropriate technology solutions, such as Enterprise Resource Planning (ERP) systems, Customer Relationship Management (CRM) systems, or Business Process Management (BPM) tools, to support process structure and enable efficient information flow.

TAXONOMY FOR SERVICE PROCESS DESIGN

		Low divergence (standardized service)			High divergence (customized service)		
		Processing of goods	Processing Information	Processing of people	Processing of goods	Processing Information	Processing of people
No Customer Contact		Dry Cleaning Restocking a vending machine	Check processing Billing for a credit card		Auto repair Tailoring a suit	Computer programming Designing a building	
Indirect customer contact			Ordering groceries from a home computer			Supervision of a landing by an air controller	
Direct Customer Contact	No customer-service worker interaction (self-service)	Operating a vending machine Assembling premade furniture	Withdrawing cash from an ATM	Operating an elevator Riding an escalator	Sampling food at a buffet dinner Bagging of groceries	Documenting medical history Searching for information in a library	Driving a rental car Using a health club facility
	Customer service worker interaction	Food service in a restaurant Hand car washing	Giving a lecture Handling routine bank transactions	Providing public transport-a tion Providing mass vaccination	Home carpet cleaning Landscaping service	Portrait painting Counseling	Haircutting Performing a surgical operation

Taxonomy refers to the classification or categorization of elements based on their characteristics or attributes. In the context of service process design, a taxonomy can be used to categorize and classify different types of service processes based on their characteristics, functions, or goals. Here is a taxonomy for service process design:

1. Core Processes: These are the primary processes that directly contribute to the creation and delivery of the core service or value proposition. They are essential for fulfilling the customers' needs and achieving the organization's strategic objectives. Examples include product development, service delivery, customer

support, and order fulfillment.

2. Support Processes: Support processes provide the necessary infrastructure and resources to enable the smooth operation of core processes. They facilitate the efficient functioning of the organization by providing support services such as human resources, finance, IT, procurement, and facilities management. Examples include recruitment, training, payroll, budgeting, and technology maintenance.

3. Customer-Facing Processes: Customer-facing processes are those that directly involve customer interactions and contribute to the customer experience. They include activities such as customer onboarding, sales, customer service, complaint handling, and relationship management. These processes focus on delivering excellent customer service, building relationships, and addressing customer needs.

4. Back-Office Processes: Back-office processes are internal processes that support the organization's operations but are not directly visible to customers. They involve administrative tasks, data management, record keeping, and internal communication. Examples include accounting, inventory management, data entry, and internal reporting. These processes ensure the smooth flow of information and resources within the organization.

5. Continuous Improvement Processes: Continuous improvement processes aim to enhance the efficiency, effectiveness, and quality of service delivery. They involve analyzing and optimizing existing processes, identifying areas

for improvement, implementing changes, and monitoring the outcomes. Examples include process mapping, performance measurement, root cause analysis, and process optimization.

GENERIC APPROACHES TO SERVICE SYSTEM DESIGN

Generic Approaches to Service Design

- Production-line
  - Limit Discretion of Personnel
  - Division of Labor
  - Substitute Technology for People
  - Standardize the Service
- Customer as Coproducer
  - Substitution of Customer Labor for Provider
  - Smoothing Service Demand
- Customer Contact
  - Degree of Customer Contact
  - Separation of High and Low Contact Operations
- Information Empowerment
  - Employee and Customer

When designing service systems, there are several generic approaches that organizations can consider. These approaches provide a framework for structuring and organizing service delivery to meet customer needs effectively. Here are some common generic approaches to service system design:

1. Self-Service Approach: In this approach, the service

system is designed to empower customers to perform service-related activities on their own, without requiring direct interaction with service personnel. Self-service options can include online portals, kiosks, mobile apps, or automated systems. This approach aims to provide convenience, efficiency, and control to customers while reducing the demand on service staff.

2. Personalization Approach: The personalization approach focuses on tailoring service experiences to individual customer preferences and needs. It involves capturing and utilizing customer data to create customized service offerings, recommendations, and experiences. Personalization can be achieved through advanced analytics, customer profiling, and leveraging technologies such as artificial intelligence and machine learning.

3. Mass Customization Approach: Mass customization combines elements of standardization and customization. It involves offering a range of standardized options that customers can customize according to their specific requirements. This approach allows organizations to efficiently deliver personalized services at scale by providing configurable options and modular service components.

4. Service Network Approach: The service network approach involves integrating multiple service providers, partners, or stakeholders to deliver a comprehensive service offering. It focuses on coordinating and orchestrating interactions and collaboration among different entities to ensure a seamless and integrated customer experience. This approach is often used in complex service ecosystems or industries with interdependent

service providers.

5. Service Ecosystem Approach: The service ecosystem approach emphasizes the interconnectedness and interdependencies of various stakeholders within the service environment. It involves designing the service system to consider the broader ecosystem of customers, suppliers, partners, and other actors. This approach recognizes the influence and impact of external factors on service delivery and aims to create value through ecosystem collaboration and co-creation.

6. Modularity Approach: The modularity approach involves breaking down the service system into modular components that can be combined and reconfigured to meet different customer needs. Each module represents a specific service offering or capability that can be easily assembled or customized. This approach allows for flexibility, scalability, and adaptation to changing customer demands.

CUSTOMER VALUE EQUATION

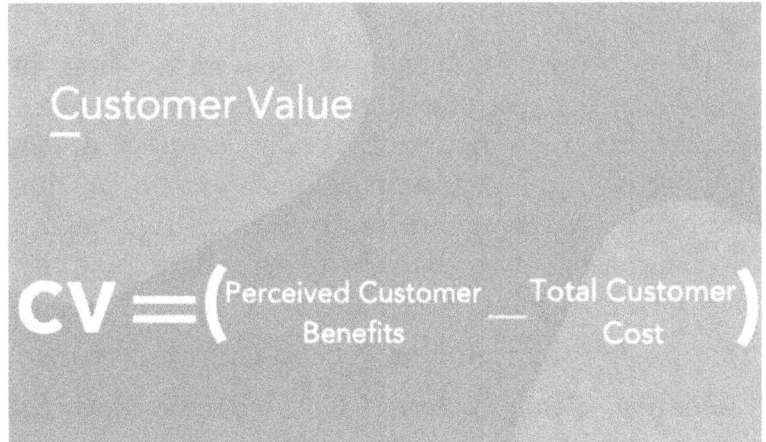

The customer value equation is a framework that helps organizations understand and quantify the value they deliver to their customers. It focuses on the exchange between the customer and the organization, considering both the benefits received by the customer and the costs incurred. The customer value equation is often expressed as:

Customer Value = Benefits Received - Costs Incurred

1. Benefits Received: This refers to the perceived value or benefits that customers derive from using a product or service. It includes both functional and emotional benefits. Functional benefits are the tangible features, capabilities, or solutions that address customer needs or problems. Emotional benefits refer to the psychological or subjective value customers experience, such as enhanced well-being, convenience, status, or enjoyment.

2. Costs Incurred: Costs represent the sacrifices or resources that customers have to invest in order to acquire and use a product or service. Costs can be monetary, such as the purchase price, ongoing fees, or maintenance costs. They can also be non-monetary, such as time, effort, inconvenience, or any negative impact experienced during the customer

journey.

The goal of the customer value equation is to ensure that the benefits received by the customer outweigh the costs incurred. When the equation results in a positive value, it indicates that the customer perceives the offering as valuable and worthwhile. On the other hand, if the equation results in a negative value, it indicates that the costs outweigh the benefits, and the customer may perceive the offering as lacking value.

Organizations can use the customer value equation as a tool to:

1. Identify Value Drivers: By understanding the elements that contribute to customer value, organizations can identify and prioritize the key value drivers that attract and retain customers. This helps in focusing resources and efforts on enhancing those aspects that have the greatest impact on customer perception of value.

2. Differentiate from Competitors: By delivering superior benefits or reducing costs for customers, organizations can create a competitive advantage. By analyzing the customer value equation, organizations can identify areas where they can differentiate themselves from competitors and create unique value propositions.

3. Optimize Pricing and Pricing Strategies: Understanding the customer value equation helps organizations in setting optimal pricing for their offerings. By aligning the price with the perceived value, organizations can ensure that customers perceive the price as fair and justifiable in relation to the benefits received.

4. Improve Customer Experience: The customer value equation helps organizations identify areas where they can improve the customer experience by enhancing benefits or reducing costs. By addressing

pain points, streamlining processes, and delivering exceptional customer service, organizations can enhance the perceived value and customer satisfaction.

5. Innovate and Develop New Offerings: The customer value equation provides insights into customer needs and preferences, helping organizations identify opportunities for innovation and the development of new products or services. By understanding the trade-off between benefits and costs, organizations can design offerings that maximize customer value.

TECHNOLOGY IN SERVICES: ROLE OF TECHNOLOGY IN THE SERVICE ENCOUNTER

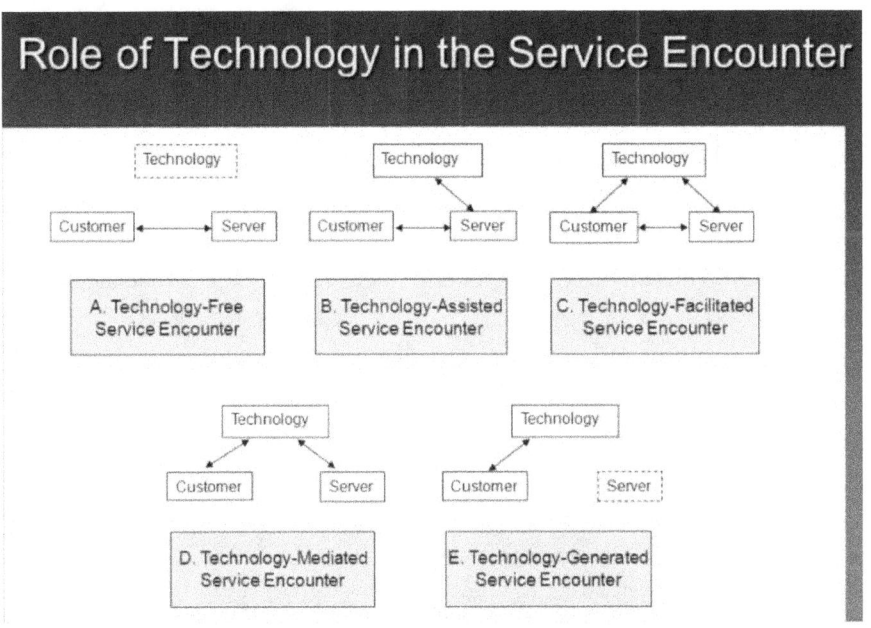

Technology plays a crucial role in shaping and enhancing the service encounter. It has the potential to transform the way services are delivered, improve customer experiences, and drive operational efficiency. Here are some key roles and benefits of technology in the service encounter:

1. Seamless Communication: Technology enables seamless communication between service providers and customers, regardless of time or location. Channels such as email, live chat, social media, and messaging apps allow customers to interact with service providers easily and receive timely responses. This improves accessibility, convenience, and responsiveness in the service encounter.

2. Self-Service Options: Technology provides self-service options that empower customers to perform service-related tasks independently. Automated systems, online portals, mobile apps, and interactive kiosks allow customers to access information, make transactions, track orders, or resolve simple issues without the need for direct interaction with service personnel. Self-service options enhance convenience, efficiency, and customer control.

3. Personalization and Customization: Technology enables the collection, analysis, and utilization of customer data to personalize and customize service encounters. Customer relationship management (CRM) systems, customer data platforms (CDPs), and advanced analytics help organizations understand individual customer preferences, purchase history, and behavior patterns. This data can be used to deliver personalized recommendations, targeted promotions, and tailored experiences that meet specific customer needs.

4. Enhanced Service Delivery: Technology facilitates the delivery of services in more efficient and effective ways. For example, automation and robotics can streamline repetitive tasks, reducing errors and improving service speed. Service management

platforms and scheduling software optimize resource allocation and coordination, ensuring that the right service provider is assigned to the right task at the right time. This enhances service quality, consistency, and operational efficiency.

5. Augmented Reality and Virtual Reality: Augmented reality (AR) and virtual reality (VR) technologies enhance the service encounter by providing immersive and interactive experiences. They can be used in various industries, such as retail, tourism, or real estate, to enable customers to visualize products, explore virtual environments, or try out virtual experiences. AR and VR technologies can help customers make more informed decisions, increase engagement, and create memorable experiences.

6. Enhanced Information Access: Technology provides easy access to information and knowledge resources during the service encounter. Service personnel can access databases, knowledge bases, or online resources to quickly retrieve information, answer customer inquiries, or provide real-time updates. This improves service accuracy, reduces response times, and enhances customer confidence in the service provider's expertise.

7. Data Analytics and Insights: Technology allows organizations to collect and analyze data from various sources to gain insights into customer preferences, behavior patterns, and service performance. This data-driven approach helps in understanding customer needs, identifying opportunities for improvement, and making data-informed decisions to enhance the service encounter. Data analytics also enables organizations to proactively anticipate customer needs, offer personalized recommendations, and provide

proactive support.

EMERGENCE OF SELF SERVICE

The emergence of self-service in various industries has been driven by advancements in technology, changing customer preferences, and the need for greater efficiency and convenience. Self-service refers to the ability of customers to perform tasks or access services independently, without the direct involvement of service personnel. Here are some key factors contributing to the emergence of self-service:

1. Technological Advancements: Advances in technology, particularly in digital and automation technologies, have enabled the development of self-service solutions. Self-service kiosks, mobile apps, online portals, and interactive voice response (IVR) systems are examples of technologies that facilitate self-service options. These technologies have become more accessible, user-friendly, and cost-effective, making self-service viable for a wide range of industries.

2. Changing Customer Preferences: Customers today value convenience, speed, and control over their service experiences. Self-service options empower customers to access services at their own convenience, bypassing queues, and time-consuming processes. It allows them to perform tasks quickly, access information instantly, and have more control over their interactions. Customers increasingly prefer self-service as it aligns with their desire for autonomy and efficiency.

3. Cost Reduction and Efficiency: Self-service can offer cost savings and operational efficiencies for businesses. By enabling customers to perform routine tasks themselves, organizations can reduce

the need for staff involvement, thereby minimizing labor costs. Self-service options can handle high volumes of transactions simultaneously, reducing waiting times and increasing service throughput. This leads to improved resource utilization and cost optimization.

4. 24/7 Accessibility: Self-service options allow customers to access services anytime, anywhere. Unlike traditional service channels that have limited operating hours, self-service solutions are available 24/7, providing customers with round-the-clock access to information and services. This accessibility enhances customer convenience and satisfaction, particularly for global businesses or customers in different time zones.

5. Customization and Personalization: Self-service solutions can be tailored to meet individual customer preferences and needs. Through personalization techniques, organizations can offer relevant recommendations, product suggestions, or targeted promotions based on customer data and behavior patterns. This customization enhances the customer experience, making self-service interactions more relevant and engaging.

6. Improved Data Collection and Analytics: Self-service transactions generate valuable data that organizations can analyze to gain insights into customer behavior, preferences, and service performance. By capturing customer data during self-service interactions, businesses can track customer journeys, identify trends, and make data-driven decisions to enhance service offerings and operational processes. Data analytics provides organizations with a better understanding of customer needs, enabling them to deliver more

targeted and personalized experiences.

7. Integration of Physical and Digital Channels: Self-service options often bridge the gap between physical and digital channels, offering a seamless customer experience. For instance, customers can start a transaction online and complete it in-store, or vice versa. This integration allows customers to switch between channels based on their preferences, providing them with flexibility and convenience.

8. COVID-19 Pandemic Impact: The COVID-19 pandemic has accelerated the adoption of self-service solutions. Physical distancing requirements and health concerns have prompted businesses to invest in contactless service options. Self-service solutions, such as mobile ordering, contactless payments, and virtual assistance, have become essential for maintaining safety and minimizing direct physical interactions.

AUTOMATION IN SERVICE

Automation in service refers to the use of technology and systems to automate manual or repetitive tasks in service delivery. It involves replacing or augmenting human effort with machines, software, or artificial intelligence to improve efficiency, accuracy, and speed. Here are some key aspects and benefits of automation in service:

1. Streamlined Processes: Automation helps streamline service processes by eliminating manual and time-consuming tasks. Routine tasks such as data entry, form filling, or order processing can be automated, reducing the likelihood of errors and speeding up service delivery. This streamlining of processes enables organizations to handle higher volumes of transactions, improve productivity, and optimize resource allocation.

2. Enhanced Efficiency and Productivity: Automation enables service providers to handle customer inquiries, requests, and transactions more efficiently. Automated systems can provide instant responses, process requests faster, and complete tasks without delays. This improves overall service speed and productivity, allowing service personnel to focus on more complex or value-added activities.

3. Consistency and Standardization: Automation ensures consistent and standardized service delivery across different interactions and touchpoints. By following predefined rules and workflows, automated systems consistently deliver the same level of service quality and adhere to established guidelines. This consistency helps build trust and reliability among customers, reducing variability in the service encounter.

4. Improved Accuracy and Error Reduction: Automation minimizes the risk of human errors in service delivery. Automated systems perform tasks with precision and accuracy, reducing the likelihood of data entry mistakes, miscalculations, or other

human errors. This leads to improved data quality, reduced rework, and enhanced service reliability.

5. Cost Reduction: Automation can result in cost savings for organizations. By automating repetitive tasks, organizations can reduce labor costs and allocate resources more efficiently. Fewer staff members may be needed to handle routine tasks, allowing organizations to optimize their workforce and focus on more value-added activities. Additionally, automation can reduce the likelihood of errors or service failures that may result in costly rework or customer dissatisfaction.

6. Enhanced Customer Experience: Automation can positively impact the customer experience by providing faster, more accurate, and convenient service. Automated systems can provide self-service options, instant responses to inquiries, and personalized recommendations based on customer data. This speeds up service delivery, reduces wait times, and offers customers greater control and convenience in accessing services.

INTERNET SERVICES

Types of Internet Services

| Communication services | File transfer services | Directory services | Ecommerce and online transactions |

| Network management services | Time services | Search engine services on the web |

Internet services refer to the various services and applications that are accessible over the internet. These services enable individuals and organizations to communicate, share information, conduct transactions, access resources, and interact with others online. Here are some common types of internet services:

1. Email: Email services allow users to send and receive messages electronically. They provide a convenient and efficient way to communicate and exchange information, both for personal and business purposes.

2. Web Browsing: Web browsing services enable users to access and navigate websites on the internet. Web browsers, such as Google Chrome, Mozilla Firefox, or Microsoft Edge, allow users to search for information, access web pages, and interact with online content.

3. Search Engines: Search engine services, such as Google, Bing, or Yahoo, help users find specific information or websites on the internet. Users can enter keywords or queries, and the search engine provides relevant search results based on its

indexing and ranking algorithms.

4. Social Media: Social media services, such as Facebook, Instagram, Twitter, LinkedIn, or Tikor, facilitate online social networking and communication. Users can create profiles, connect with others, share content, and engage in discussions or interactions within the social media platforms.

5. Online Communication: Internet services provide various means of online communication, including instant messaging (e.g., WhatsApp, Facebook Messenger), video conferencing (e.g., Zoom, Microsoft Teams), voice over IP (e.g., Skype, Google Voice), and online forums or discussion boards.

6. Online Shopping and E-commerce: E-commerce services enable users to purchase products or services online. Online marketplaces, such as Amazon or eBay, allow users to browse and buy a wide range of products, while online payment services, such as PayPal or Stripe, facilitate secure transactions.

7. Streaming Services: Streaming services, such as Netflix, Spotify, or YouTube, deliver multimedia content over the internet. Users can stream movies, TV shows, music, or videos on-demand, without the need for downloading or physical media.

8. Cloud Computing: Cloud computing services provide on-demand access to computing resources and storage over the internet. Users can store and access data, run applications, and leverage computing power without the need for physical infrastructure.

9. Online Banking and Financial Services: Internet services enable online banking and financial transactions. Users can access their accounts,

transfer funds, pay bills, or manage investments through online banking platforms or financial service providers.

10. Online Education and E-Learning: Internet services support online education and e-learning platforms. Users can access educational resources, participate in virtual classrooms, and engage in distance learning programs.

11. Online Content and Media Publishing: Internet services facilitate the creation, publishing, and sharing of online content. Users can create blogs, websites, or multimedia content and share them with a global audience.

12. Web Hosting and Domain Services: Internet services include web hosting and domain registration services, which enable individuals and organizations to host websites and register domain names for their online presence.

ELECTRONIC AND TRADITIONAL SERVICES

Electronic and Traditional Services

Features	Electronic	Traditional
Service Encounter	Screen-to-face	Face-to-face
Availability	Anytime	Standard working hours
Access	From home	Travel to location
Market Area	Worldwide	Local
Ambiance	Electronic interface	Physical environment
Privacy	Anonymity	Social interaction

Electronic services and traditional services refer to different modes or channels through which services are delivered to customers. Here's a comparison between electronic services and traditional services:

Electronic Services:

1. Delivery Channel: Electronic services are delivered through digital platforms and technology, primarily over the internet. Customers access and interact with these services using computers, smartphones, or other connected devices.

2. Accessibility and Convenience: Electronic services offer high accessibility and convenience. Customers can access these services anytime and anywhere with an internet connection. They can perform tasks, access information, and conduct transactions at their own convenience without being restricted by physical location or operating hours.

3. Speed and Efficiency: Electronic services are often faster and more efficient compared to traditional

services. Transactions can be completed quickly, information can be accessed instantaneously, and processes can be automated, reducing the need for manual intervention. This speed and efficiency save time and effort for both customers and service providers.

4. Automation and Self-Service: Electronic services often incorporate automation and self-service elements. Customers can perform tasks independently without the need for direct human interaction. Examples include online banking, self-checkout systems, or automated customer support through chatbots.

5. Scalability and Global Reach: Electronic services have the potential for high scalability and global reach. They can handle a large number of transactions simultaneously and can easily reach customers around the world. This scalability allows organizations to expand their customer base and serve a larger audience without significant physical infrastructure investments.

6. Personalization and Data-driven Insights: Electronic services leverage customer data to personalize experiences and offer targeted recommendations. Organizations can gather and analyze data on customer preferences, behavior, and purchase history to deliver personalized content, recommendations, or promotions. These data-driven insights enable organizations to better understand customer needs and enhance the overall customer experience.

Traditional Services:

1. In-Person Interaction: Traditional services involve direct in-person interaction between customers and

service providers. These services are delivered in physical locations such as stores, offices, or service centers, where customers can interact face-to-face with service personnel.

2. Tangible Elements: Traditional services often involve tangible elements such as physical products, facilities, or materials. For example, a customer visiting a salon for a haircut receives the service in a physical space and interacts with tangible tools and equipment.

3. Personal Touch and Relationship Building: Traditional services offer a personal touch and the opportunity for service providers to build relationships with customers. Direct interaction allows for personalized communication, understanding of customer needs, and customization of services based on individual preferences.

4. Limited Operating Hours: Traditional services are often limited by operating hours and physical location. Customers can only access services during specific hours when the service provider is open. This may restrict accessibility for customers with busy schedules or those located far from service locations.

5. Physical Queues and Waiting Times: Traditional services may involve physical queues and waiting times. Customers may need to wait in line for service, leading to potential frustration or dissatisfaction if wait times are long. Service providers must manage queues effectively to minimize customer wait times.

6. Limited Geographical Reach: Traditional services are often localized and have limited geographical

reach. They are tied to physical locations, making it challenging to serve customers who are located far away. Expansion into new markets may require establishing new physical locations or branches.

SERVICE PRODUCT AND PROCESS DIMENSIONS

Service Product Dimensions:

1. Core Product: The core product dimension represents the basic benefit or value that customers seek from a service. It is the primary reason customers engage with a service and the fundamental problem or need that the service addresses. For example, the core product of a healthcare service is medical treatment or care.

2. Supplementary Services: Supplementary services are additional elements that enhance the core product and provide additional value to customers. These services may include customer support, delivery, installation, maintenance, warranties, or customization options. Supplementary services complement the core product and help differentiate the service offering.

3. Service Features: Service features refer to the specific characteristics, functionalities, or attributes of the service that differentiate it from competitors. Features can include aspects such as speed, reliability, convenience, quality, variety, or personalization. Service features help create a unique selling proposition and attract customers.

4. Service Quality: Service quality represents the overall excellence or level of performance that customers perceive in a service. It encompasses factors such as responsiveness, reliability, assurance, empathy, and tangibles (physical evidence). Service

quality is a critical dimension that impacts customer satisfaction and loyalty.

Service Process Dimensions:

1. Customer Involvement: Customer involvement refers to the extent of customer participation or co-production in the service delivery process. It can range from low involvement, where customers have minimal interaction, to high involvement, where customers actively participate in the creation of the service. Customer involvement impacts the customer experience and the efficiency of service delivery.

2. Service Delivery Channels: Service delivery channels represent the means or methods through which services are delivered to customers. Channels can include face-to-face interactions, online platforms, mobile applications, call centers, self-service kiosks, or a combination of these. The choice of delivery channels impacts accessibility, convenience, and customer preferences.

3. Service Flow and Sequencing: Service flow and sequencing refer to the sequence of activities and steps involved in delivering the service. It includes the order in which tasks are performed, the coordination among different service providers, and the overall flow of the service process. Efficient flow and sequencing ensure smooth service delivery and minimize delays or bottlenecks.

4. Service Customization: Service customization represents the ability to tailor or personalize the service to meet individual customer needs or preferences. It involves adapting the service to specific customer requirements, offering flexible options, and providing personalized

recommendations. Service customization enhances customer satisfaction and creates a more personalized experience.

5. Service Time and Duration: Service time and duration refer to the amount of time required to deliver the service and the duration of the service encounter. It includes factors such as waiting times, service speed, and overall time efficiency. Managing service time and duration is crucial in meeting customer expectations and optimizing resource utilization.

6. Service Employee Interaction: Service employee interaction represents the interactions and engagement between service employees and customers during the service encounter. It encompasses factors such as employee behavior, communication, knowledge, and responsiveness. Positive employee interactions contribute to customer satisfaction, trust, and the overall service experience.

TECHNOLOGICAL INNOVATION IN SERVICES

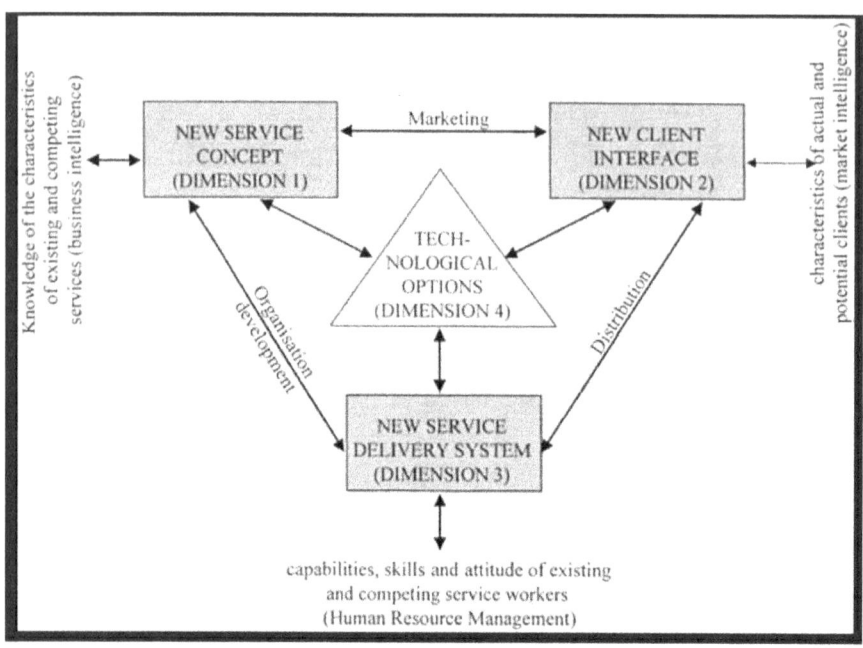

Technological innovation in services refers to the development and adoption of new technologies and digital solutions to improve service delivery, enhance customer experiences, and drive operational efficiencies in service-oriented industries. Here are some key areas where technological innovation has had a significant impact:

1. Automation and Artificial Intelligence (AI): Automation and AI technologies have transformed service delivery by replacing or augmenting human tasks with machines and algorithms. Chatbots, virtual assistants, and robotic process automation (RPA) streamline customer interactions and back-office processes, improving efficiency and response times. AI-powered algorithms enable personalized recommendations, predictive analytics, and advanced data analysis to enhance service experiences.

2. Digital Platforms and Mobile Apps: Digital platforms and mobile applications have revolutionized how

services are accessed and delivered. These platforms provide convenient and user-friendly interfaces for customers to access services, make transactions, track orders, or seek support. They enable seamless communication, personalized experiences, and self-service options, enhancing convenience and accessibility.

3. Internet of Things (IoT): The IoT connects physical devices and objects to the internet, enabling data collection, monitoring, and control. In service industries, IoT technology is used to gather real-time data on equipment performance, inventory levels, or environmental conditions. This data is then leveraged to optimize service delivery, proactively identify maintenance needs, or trigger automated actions.

4. Cloud Computing: Cloud computing enables organizations to store, process, and access data and applications remotely over the internet. Cloud-based solutions provide scalable infrastructure, data storage, and computing power without the need for on-premises hardware. Service providers leverage cloud computing to offer on-demand services, ensure data security, and facilitate collaboration and data sharing.

5. Big Data and Analytics: Big data and analytics enable organizations to collect, analyze, and derive insights from large volumes of structured and unstructured data. In service industries, data analytics is used to understand customer behavior, identify trends, personalize offerings, and optimize service processes. It helps in making data-driven decisions, improving operational efficiency, and enhancing customer experiences.

6. Augmented Reality (AR) and Virtual Reality (VR): AR and VR technologies create immersive and interactive experiences that enhance service encounters. In sectors like retail, tourism, or real estate, AR and VR enable customers to visualize products, explore virtual environments, or receive virtual guidance. These technologies provide a richer and more engaging experience, aiding in decision-making and reducing physical constraints.

CHAPTER 3

Service Quality:

Service quality is a critical aspect of any business that provides services to its customers. It refers to the level of excellence or superiority exhibited by a company in fulfilling the needs and expectations of its clientele. A high level of service quality is essential for customer satisfaction, loyalty, and the overall success of the business. In this note, we will explore the key components of service quality, its importance, and strategies for enhancing it.

Service quality (SQ), in its contemporary conceptualization, is a comparison of perceived expectations (E) of a service with perceived performance (P), giving rise to the equation $SQ = P - E$

Evolution of service quality concept

Historically, scholars have treated service quality as very difficult to define and measure, due to the inherent intangible nature of services, which are often experienced subjectively.

One of the earliest attempts to grapple with the service quality concept came from the so-called *Nordic School*. In this approach, service quality was seen as having two basic dimensions:

Technical quality: What the customer receives as a result of interactions with the service firm (e.g. a meal in a restaurant, a bed in a hotel)

Functional quality: *How* the customer receives the service; the expressive nature of the service delivery (e.g. courtesy, attentiveness, promptness)

The technical quality is relatively objective and therefore easy to measure. However, difficulties arise when trying to evaluate functional quality.

Importance of Service Quality:

1. Customer Satisfaction: Service quality is directly linked to customer satisfaction. Satisfied customers are more likely to become loyal patrons, leading to repeat business and positive word-of-mouth recommendations.

2. Customer Loyalty: High service quality fosters trust and loyalty in customers, making it less likely for them to switch to competitors even if they offer lower prices.

3. Brand Reputation: Excellent service quality can significantly enhance a company's reputation and brand image. Positive reviews and feedback from satisfied customers can attract new clients and strengthen the existing customer base.

4. Competitive Advantage: In today's highly competitive market, service quality can be a crucial differentiator. A business that consistently provides superior service is likely to gain a competitive edge over its rivals.

Strategies to Improve Service Quality:

1. Employee Training: Invest in comprehensive training programs to equip employees with the necessary skills and knowledge to deliver exceptional service.

2. Customer Feedback: Regularly gather customer feedback through surveys, reviews, and direct interactions to identify areas for improvement and to address customer concerns.

3. Service Recovery: Develop effective protocols for

handling customer complaints and resolving issues promptly and satisfactorily.

4. Process Optimization: Continuously review and optimize service delivery processes to ensure efficiency and effectiveness.

5. Recognize and Reward Excellence: Acknowledge and reward employees who consistently deliver outstanding service to motivate others to follow suit.

Dimensions of Service Quality

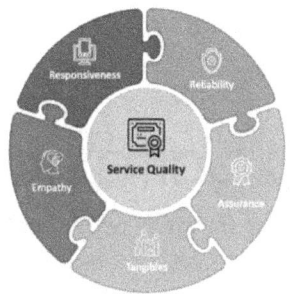

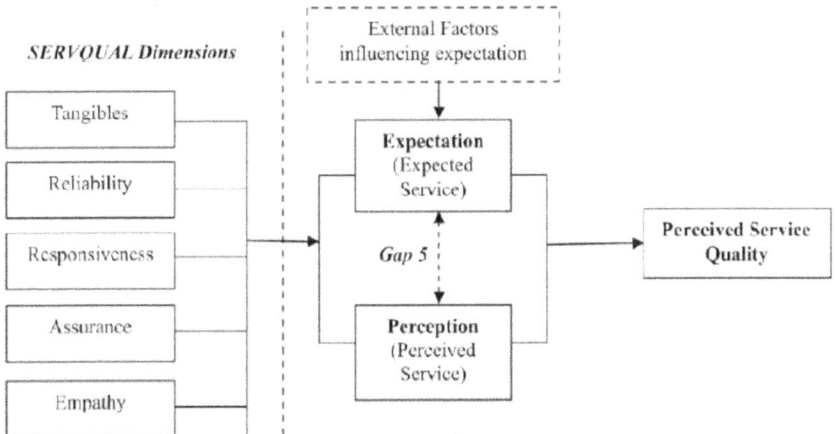

A customer's expectation of a particular service is determined by factors such as recommendations, personal needs and past experiences. The expected service and the perceived service sometimes may not be equal, thus leaving a gap. The service quality model or the 'GAP model' developed in 1985, highlights the main requirements for delivering high service quality. It identifies five 'gaps' that cause unsuccessful delivery. Customers generally have a tendency to compare the service they 'experience' with the service they 'expect'. If the experience does not match the expectation, there arises a gap. Given the emphasis on expectations, this approach to measuring service quality is known as the *expectancy-disconfirmation paradigm* and is the dominant model in the consumer behaviour and marketing literature.

A model of service quality, based on the expectancy-disconformation paradigm, and developed by A. Parasuraman, Valarie A. Zeithaml and Len Berry, identifies the principal dimensions (or components) of service quality and proposes a scale for measuring service quality, known as SERVQUAL. The model's developers originally identified ten dimensions of service quality that influence customer's perceptions of service quality. However, after extensive testing and retesting, some of the dimensions were found to be auto correlated and the total number of dimensions was reduced to five, namely - reliability, assurance, tangibles, empathy and responsiveness. These five dimensions are thought to represent the dimensions of service quality across a range of industries and settings. Among students of marketing, the mnemonic, **RATER**, an acronym formed from the first letter of each of the five dimensions, is often used as an aid to recall.

In spite of the dominance of the expectancy-disconfirmation paradigm, scholars have questioned its validity. In particular scholars have pointed out the expectancy-disconfirmation approach had its roots in consumer research and was fundamentally concerned with measuring customer satisfaction rather than service quality. In other words, questions surround the *face validity* of the model and whether service quality can be conceptualized as a *gap*.

Service quality is commonly assessed and measured using

various dimensions or factors that help evaluate the overall performance and excellence of a service. Some of the most widely recognized dimensions of service quality are:

1. Reliability: Reliability refers to the ability of a service provider to consistently and accurately deliver its promised service or perform its duties without errors or delays. Customers expect reliability in terms of meeting deadlines, keeping appointments, and fulfilling commitments made by the service provider.

2. Responsiveness: Responsiveness pertains to the promptness and willingness of the service provider to address customer inquiries, requests, and concerns. A responsive service provider shows attentiveness and empathy towards customers' needs, thereby enhancing customer satisfaction.

3. Assurance: Assurance reflects the knowledge, competence, and courtesy of the service provider and its employees. Customers need to feel confident that they are dealing with skilled professionals who can handle their requests competently and provide accurate information.

4. Empathy: Empathy involves understanding and demonstrating care for customers' individual needs and circumstances. Service providers who display empathy can build stronger emotional connections with customers, leading to increased customer loyalty.

5. Tangibles: Tangibles encompass the physical aspects of the service that customers can observe and touch. This includes the appearance of facilities, equipment, and other materials used to provide the service. Tangibles contribute to the overall perception of service quality.

6. Assurance: Assurance involves building trust and confidence in customers by displaying expertise, reliability, and consistency in service delivery. It is closely related to the competence and professionalism of the service provider and its employees.

7. Credibility: Credibility relates to the believability and trustworthiness of the service provider. It involves the company's reputation, track record, and the customer's perception of its ability to deliver the promised service as expected.

8. Security: Security pertains to the customer's sense of safety and protection when using the service. For certain services, such as financial transactions or data handling, ensuring robust security measures is crucial for gaining customer trust.

Measuring Service Quality

Measuring service quality may involve both subjective and objective processes. In both cases, it is often some aspect of customer satisfaction which is being assessed. However, customer satisfaction is an indirect measure of service quality. Research has also indicated that the presence of service quality leads to several outcomes including changes in perceived value, customer satisfaction and loyalty intentions with consumers.

Measuring subjective elements of service quality

Subjective processes can be assessed in characteristics (assessed be the SERVQUAL method); in incidents (assessed in critical incident theory) and in problems (assessed by *Frequenz Relevanz Analyse* a German term. The most important and most used method with which to measure subjective elements of service quality is the Servqual method.

Measuring objective elements of service quality

Objective processes may be subdivided into primary processes and secondary processes. During primary processes, silent customers create test episodes of service or the service episodes of normal customers are observed. In secondary processes, quantifiable factors such as numbers of customer complaints or numbers of returned goods are analyzed in order to make inferences about service quality.

SERVQUAL The most widely-used measure for service quality has been the 'SERVQUAL' measure of Parasuraman, Zeithaml and Berry, according to which customer assessment of service quality results from a comparison of service expectations and actual performance.

It measures the service quality on the five service quality dimensions discussed earlier in this unit viz. Reliability, Responsiveness, Assurance, Empathy and Tangibles. Reliability largely concerns whether the outcome of service delivery was as promised. The other four dimensions relate to the process of service delivery or how the service was delivered. Servqual scores are expressed as the difference between expectations and perceptions i.e. it measures the gap between the service that customer think should be provided and what they think actually has been provided. Respondents complete a series of scale, which measure their expectations on five service quality dimensions and subsequently, they are asked to record their perceptions of that company's performance on those same dimensions. When perceived performance ratings are lower than expectations this is sign of poor quality; the reverse indicates good quality.

Example:

A) Expectation Statements (E)

• The physical facilities at banks should be visually appealing

Strongly Disagree   Strongly Agree

1   2   3   4   5
6   7

● Banks should give customers individual attention

Strongly Disagree   Strongly Agree

1   2   3   4   5
6   7

B) Corresponding Perception Statements (P)

● The physical facilities at XYZ Bank are visually appealing

Strongly Disagree   Strongly Agree

1   2   3   4   5
6   7

XYZ bank gives customers individual attention

Strongly Disagree   Strongly Agree

1   2   3   4   5
6   7

The original SERVQUAL instrument consisted of 22 statements covering the five service quality dimensions (4 questions on tangibles, 5 on reliability, 4 on responsiveness, 4 on assurance and 5 on empathy) - i.e. a set of 22 statements covering expectations and a set of 22 corresponding statements covering perceptions. Expectations and perceptions statements includes aspects like (i) equipments, physical facilities, appearance of employees, materials associated with the service like pamphlets or statements (tangibles) ii) timely provision of service, performing the service right the first time, meeting the promises, sincere interest in solving the problems (reliability), (iii) prompt service, willingness to help, employees never too busy to respond to customer requests (responsiveness), (iv) behaviour of employees instilling confidence, feeling of safety in transactions, employees having knowledge to answer the questions (assurance) and (v) individual attention to customers, employees understanding specific needs of customers (empathy). In addition to expectations and perceptions section the SERVQUAL contained a "point allocating question" which was used to ascertain the relative importance of the five dimensions by asking respondents to allocate a total of 100 points among the dimensions.

The SERVQUAL scale can be used

i) To determine a company's service quality along each of the five service quality dimensions.

ii) To find out relative importance of service quality dimensions as considered by the customer.

iii) To compute overall weighted SERVQUAL score - this takes into account the relative importance of each dimension as well.

iv) To track customers' expectations and perception over time

v) To compare a company's SERVQUAL score against those of competitors

E-Service Quality - The concept of "eservice" emerged from the growth of the internet and its application in business. Zeithaml et al. defined e-service quality as the extent to which a website facilitates efficient and effective shopping, purchasing and delivery of services. In the view of Parasuraman et al. e-service quality involves all phases of a customer's interactions with a website. To further understand the nature of e-services, Zeithaml et al. reviewed the gap model of service quality and proposed the gap model of e-service quality.

DIMENSIONS OF E-SERVICE QUALITY

S/N	Author(s)	Year	Study	Dimensions of E-Service Quality Used
1	Zeithaml et al.	2000	Online Shopping	Reliability, Responsiveness, Access, Flexibility, Ease of navigation, Efficiency, Assurance/trust, Security/privacy, Price knowledge, Site aesthetics and Customisation/personalisation
2	Santos	2003	E-Commerce	Incubative dimensions: Web appearance, Ease of use, Linkage layout, Content Active dimensions: Reliability, Efficiency, Security, Support, Communication, Incentive
3	Bauer et al.	2006	Online Shopping	Functionality/design, Reliability, Process, Responsiveness, Enjoyment
4	Hongxiu et al.	2009	Online travel service	Ease of use, Website design, Reliability, Service availability, Privacy, Responsiveness, Empathy
5	Alsudairi	2012	E-Banking	Accessibility, Usability, Functional usefulness, Safety, Convenience, Responsiveness, Realisation
6	Narteh	2015	ATM	Convenience, Reliability, Ease of Use, Privacy and Security, Responsiveness, Fulfilment
7	Tan et al.	2018	Internet Retail Service	Information, Navigation, Security, Responsiveness, Reliability
8	Nihayah et al.	2021	E-Banking	Accessibility, Responsiveness, Functional usefulness, Usability, Safety, Convenience, Realisation

Other Measures - Apart from conducting customer surveys like the one using SERVQUAL as described above, some of the other methods which service organizations use to obtain information about their service quality are briefly explained below:

a) Transaction Surveys: This type of research involves tracking the information about customer or all of the key service encounters with the customer. These surveys are also called 'trailer calls' or 'post transaction surveys'. This is usually done with the help of a small questionnaire immediately after a service transaction has taken place e.g. survey of airlines passengers while disembarking or that of a hotel guest while checking out. These surveys also provide the management a tool for monitoring the performance of individual service contact personnel.

b) Complaint Solicitation and Analysis: Customers tend to voice their dissatisfaction through complaints. An analysis of the complaints can help in identifying quality failure points.

c) Mystery Shopping: In this method outside research companies are used by the service organization who send people posing as customers in order to judge the service quality. The mystery shopper is unknown to the service provider. This is a popular method in the retail sector. Mystery shopping, also termed as Ghost Shopping, can be a very effective way of reinforcing service quality standards.

d) Asking Customers: This involves asking customers directly what they would like to be done to increase the quality of service and their satisfaction. This can be very effective in business - to - business situation. This primarily concerns with the expectation aspect. A slight variation of this, which includes perceptions about the service quality as well is to form customer panels i.e. ongoing groups of customers who are assembled to provide perceptions about a service over a period of time.

e) Intermediary Research: This form of research is useful in services where intermediaries form an important part of the service delivery process and have a major direct contact with customers. In such situation intermediaries can provide valuable feedback to the service firm regarding quality of service as perceived by the customers.

Quality Service by Design

"Quality Service by Design" is a concept that emphasizes the intentional and proactive approach to delivering excellent service. It involves designing and implementing service processes, systems, and practices with the primary goal of ensuring high-quality service experiences for customers. The idea is to integrate service quality considerations into every aspect of the organization's operations and culture.

Key elements of "Quality Service by Design" include:

1. Customer-Centric Approach: Putting the customer at the center of service design is fundamental. Understanding customer needs, preferences, and

pain points is essential for creating services that truly address and exceed customer expectations.

2. Service Design Thinking: Applying design thinking principles to service design allows businesses to creatively and collaboratively develop innovative service solutions. This involves empathizing with customers, defining their problems, ideating potential solutions, prototyping, and testing them to achieve the best results.

3. Process Optimization: Adopting continuous process improvement methodologies, such as Six Sigma or Lean, helps optimize service processes to reduce inefficiencies and errors, resulting in smoother, more consistent service delivery.

4. Employee Training and Engagement: Empowering employees with the necessary skills, knowledge, and authority to provide exceptional service is crucial. Organizations should invest in comprehensive training programs to enhance employee competencies and encourage a customer-centric mindset.

5. Service Recovery Planning: Even with meticulous planning, service failures can occur. Implementing a robust service recovery plan allows companies to respond swiftly and effectively to customer complaints or issues, turning negative experiences into positive ones.

6. Feedback and Measurement: Regularly seeking customer feedback and measuring key service quality metrics are vital for understanding the impact of service design efforts. Data-driven insights help identify strengths and areas for improvement.

7. Consistency and Standardization: Standardizing service delivery processes ensures consistency

across different touchpoints and interactions. This consistency builds trust and confidence in customers, knowing that they will receive a similar level of service each time they engage with the company.

8. Empowering Frontline Employees: Providing frontline employees with decision-making authority and autonomy enables them to make real-time decisions to resolve customer issues promptly and enhance the overall service experience.

Perceived Service Quality

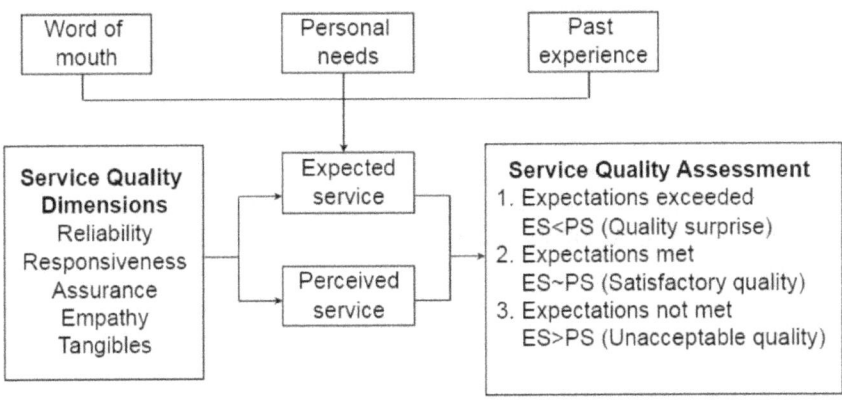

Service Quality Gap Analysis

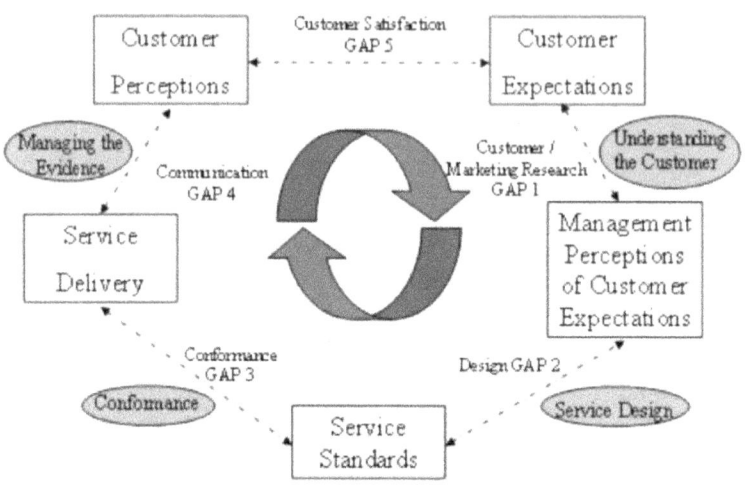

Quality Service by Design

- **Quality in the Service Package**
  - Supporting facility
  - Facilitating goods
  - Information
  - Explicit services
  - Implicit services
- **Taguchi methods (robust design)**
- **Poka-yoke (fail-safing)**
  - Example: Height bar at amusement park
- **Quality Function Deployment**
  - House of Quality
- **Walk-Through Audit**

Walk Through Audit

Walk through audit is a customer-focused survey to find the areas for improvement

- Entire customer experience is traced from beginning to end, and a flow chart of customer interaction with service system is made

- Customer is asked for his/her impressions on each of these interactions

A walk-through audit in service quality is a systematic examination of various aspects of a service delivery process, customer interactions, and service environment to assess the overall quality of the service experience. This type of audit helps organizations identify strengths and areas for improvement, ultimately leading to enhanced customer satisfaction and loyalty. Here's a step-by-step guide on conducting a walk-through audit in service quality:

1. Define Objectives: Clearly outline the objectives of the service quality walk-through audit. Determine what aspects of the service experience you want to evaluate, such as service responsiveness, employee behavior, service environment, or service process efficiency.

2. Plan the Walk-Through: Develop a plan that outlines the service touchpoints and customer interactions that will be audited. If possible, involve employees from different departments who are directly involved in the service delivery process.

3. Conduct the Walk-Through: Start the walk-through audit by interacting with the service from a customer's perspective. Move through various customer touchpoints and assess the service experience, including service encounters, waiting

areas, signage, and customer service channels (e.g., phone, email, chat).

4. Observe Employee Interactions: Pay close attention to how employees interact with customers. Observe their demeanor, communication skills, problem-solving abilities, and adherence to service standards.

5. Assess Service Environment: Evaluate the physical environment where the service is delivered, such as the cleanliness, comfort, and overall ambiance of the service area.

6. Evaluate Service Processes: Analyze the efficiency and effectiveness of service processes, from the moment a customer initiates contact to the resolution of their query or request.

7. Measure Service Responsiveness: Assess the speed and effectiveness of the service provider's response to customer inquiries, complaints, or requests for assistance.

8. Interview Employees: Engage in discussions with service employees to gain insights into their perspectives on service quality, challenges they face, and potential solutions.

9. Analyze the Data: After completing the walk-through audit, analyze the collected data to identify patterns, recurring issues, and opportunities for improvement.

10. Prepare the Audit Report: Compile the audit findings, recommendations, and any supporting documentation into a comprehensive audit report. Clearly communicate the results and proposed actions to relevant stakeholders, including management and frontline employees.

11. Implement Improvements: Collaborate with

relevant teams to implement the recommended improvements, and monitor the impact of these changes on service quality over time.

Achieving Service Quality

Achieving service quality in service operations management (OM) involves implementing effective strategies and practices that focus on delivering exceptional service experiences to customers. Here are some key steps to achieve service quality in service OM:

1. Customer-Centric Approach: Put the customer at the center of service operations. Understand their needs, preferences, and expectations through customer feedback, surveys, and market research.

2. Service Design and Process Mapping: Design service processes that are efficient, effective, and customer-friendly. Map out the customer journey and identify touchpoints where service quality can be enhanced.

3. Standardization and Service Standards: Establish clear service standards and guidelines for employees to follow. Standardizing processes ensures consistency and helps maintain service quality across different interactions.

4. Employee Training and Development: Invest in training programs to equip employees with the necessary skills and knowledge to deliver high-quality service. Provide ongoing development opportunities to keep employees up-to-date with industry trends and best practices.

5. Service Level Agreements (SLAs): If applicable, create SLAs that outline specific performance metrics and targets for service delivery. SLAs help set clear expectations and hold service providers accountable for meeting customer requirements.

6. Technology Integration: Leverage technology to enhance service efficiency and quality. Implement customer relationship management (CRM) systems, service automation, and data analytics tools to improve service delivery.

7. Feedback and Performance Measurement: Implement a system to gather customer feedback and measure service performance. Key performance indicators (KPIs) can help monitor service quality and identify areas for improvement.

8. Continuous Improvement: Foster a culture of continuous improvement within the service operations. Encourage employees to contribute ideas for enhancing service quality and efficiency.

9. Cross-Functional Collaboration: Encourage collaboration between different departments and teams involved in service delivery. Effective communication and coordination improve overall service quality.

10. Benchmarking and Best Practices: Benchmark service quality against industry standards and best practices. Learn from successful service organizations and adapt proven strategies to your specific context.

Service Recovery

Service recovery is the process of addressing and resolving customer complaints, issues, or problems in a prompt and effective manner to restore customer satisfaction and loyalty. Despite a company's best efforts, service failures or mistakes can happen. When they do, service recovery becomes crucial in turning a negative customer experience into a positive one.

The Service Recovery Paradox

The service recovery paradox refers to the phenomenon where a customer who has experienced a service failure and had the issue effectively resolved through service recovery ends up being more satisfied and loyal than if they had not experienced any service failure at all. In other words, a well-handled service recovery situation can lead to a stronger customer relationship and higher customer satisfaction levels than if there had been no problem in the first place.tr

Key Elements of Service Recovery:

1. Swift Response: Time is of the essence in service recovery. Acknowledge the customer's concern promptly and let them know that their feedback is being taken seriously.

2. Active Listening: Empathize with the customer's frustration or disappointment and actively listen to their concerns without interruption. Understanding the customer's perspective is essential in finding an appropriate solution.

3. Apology: Sincerely apologize for the inconvenience or negative experience the customer has faced. A genuine apology goes a long way in expressing concern and regret for the issue.

4. Resolution: Resolve the customer's issue to the best of your ability. Offer solutions that are tailored to the specific situation and provide options to address the problem.

5. Compensation: Depending on the severity of the issue, consider offering compensation, such as refunds, discounts, or complimentary services. This gesture can demonstrate the company's commitment to making things right.

6. Follow-Up: After resolving the issue, follow up with the customer to ensure their satisfaction and to show that their feedback is valued.

Benefits of Effective Service Recovery:

1. Customer Retention: Properly handled service recovery can lead to customer retention. Customers who have their issues resolved are more likely to remain loyal to the company.

2. Customer Loyalty: Service recovery efforts can strengthen customer loyalty. Satisfied customers are more likely to become brand advocates and recommend the company to others.

3. Positive Word-of-Mouth: Customers who experience effective service recovery are more likely to share their positive experiences with friends, family, and colleagues, which can lead to new customers.

4. Reputation Management: Demonstrating a commitment to service recovery can positively impact the company's reputation and brand image.

5. Employee Morale: Empowering employees to handle service recovery can boost their morale and job satisfaction, as they feel supported and trusted by the company.

6. Continuous Improvement: Analyzing service

recovery cases can provide insights into areas for improvement in service delivery and processes.

Stages in Quality Development

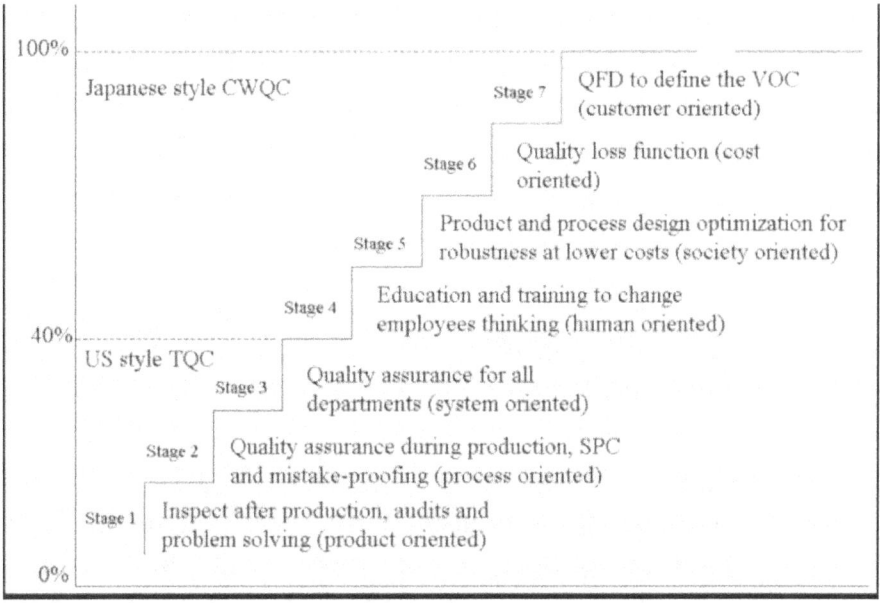

Stage 1: Inspection: The first stage involves quality inspection, where products or services are checked for defects and conformity to established standards. Inspection is an early form of quality control, where a sample of the output is tested to identify defects.

1. Stage 2: Quality Assurance: Moving beyond inspection, quality assurance focuses on preventing defects rather than merely identifying them. This stage involves setting up processes and systems to ensure that products or services consistently meet quality standards. Quality assurance aims to build quality into the processes from the beginning.

2. Stage 3: Quality for All (Employee Involvement): Quality for All refers to the stage where the concept of quality becomes a shared responsibility across

all employees in the organization. It emphasizes employee involvement and engagement in the pursuit of quality excellence.

3. Stage 4: Design Optimization: Design optimization involves designing products or services with quality in mind from the outset. It aims to reduce the chances of defects by improving the design, ensuring ease of use, and considering customer needs during the design process.

4. Stage 5: Education and Training: Education and training are critical components of quality development. At this stage, employees receive relevant training to enhance their skills, knowledge, and understanding of quality principles and techniques.

5. Stage 6: Quality Loss Function: The Quality Loss Function, introduced by Genichi Taguchi, is a statistical concept that quantifies the financial loss caused by deviations from a target value or specification. It emphasizes minimizing variation around the target value to reduce quality-related costs.

6. Stage 7: Quality Function Deployment (QFD): Quality Function Deployment is a systematic approach used to translate customer needs and expectations into specific product or service design requirements. QFD aims to ensure that customer needs are at the forefront of the design and development process.

The service encounter:

The service encounter, also known as the moment of truth, refers to the interaction between a customer and a service provider during the delivery of a service. It is a critical moment that significantly influences the customer's perception of the service and the overall service experience. The service encounter is a key determinant of customer satisfaction, loyalty, and the success of the service provider.

From the customer's point of view, the most vivid impression of service occurs in the **service encounters or "Moment of Truth**," when the customer interacts with the service firm. This is the foundation to "Satisfaction of Service Quality" — it is where the promises are kept or broken. The concept of **service encounter** was put forth by Richard Norman, taking the metaphor from Bull Fighting. Most services are results of social acts, which take place in direct contact between the customer and the service provider. At this stage the customer realizes the perceived service quality.

Key characteristics of the service encounter include:

1. Direct Interaction: The service encounter involves direct face-to-face or virtual interaction between the customer and the service provider. It can take place in various settings, such as a retail store, a restaurant, a call center, or an online chat platform.

2. Customer Experience: The service encounter shapes the customer's experience with the service. It includes all aspects of the customer-provider interaction, from the initial greeting to the resolution of the customer's inquiry or request.

3. Moment of Truth: The service encounter is often referred to as the moment of truth because it is when the customer's expectations meet the actual service performance. It can either lead to customer delight or disappointment, depending on how well the service provider meets customer needs and

demands.

4. Emotional Impact: The service encounter can evoke strong emotions in customers. Positive encounters can create feelings of satisfaction, trust, and loyalty, while negative encounters can result in frustration, anger, and dissatisfaction.

5. Customer Perception: The customer's perception of the service encounter is influenced by various factors, including the behavior and attitude of the service provider, the efficiency of service delivery, and the overall atmosphere or ambiance of the service environment.

6. Customer Interaction Points: The service encounter includes multiple touchpoints where customers interact with the service provider, such as greetings, problem-solving conversations, payment transactions, and farewells.

7. Importance of Service Recovery: In cases where the service encounter falls short of customer expectations or errors occur, effective service recovery becomes crucial. Addressing customer complaints or issues promptly and satisfactorily can turn a negative encounter into a positive one.

8. Role of Service Employees: Frontline service employees play a vital role in shaping the service encounter. Their behavior, communication skills, product knowledge, and responsiveness significantly impact the customer's experience.

9. Moments of Delight: A well-handled service encounter can create moments of delight for customers. These positive experiences can lead to increased customer loyalty, positive word-of-mouth, and repeat business.

Type of Service Encounter	Description	Examples
Face-to-Face Encounters	Direct, in-person interactions between customer and service provider	Retail store sales, restaurant dining, healthcare
Remote Encounters	Customer interacts with the provider through communication channels	Customer support calls, online chats, video calls
Self-Service Encounters	Customer performs the service task independently	Self-checkout kiosks, online order placement
Automated Encounters	Interaction with fully automated systems or technology	IVR systems, chatbots, automated account services
Co-Creation Encounters	Active collaboration between customer and provider for a custom experience	Personal training, travel planning, customized products
High-Touch Encounters	Requires significant interpersonal interaction and personal attention	Luxury spa treatments, personalized financial planning
Low-Touch Encounters	Minimal personal interaction; brief and straightforward	Supermarket checkout, vending machine use
Social Media Encounters	Customer interactions with companies on social media platforms	Reviews, inquiries, support through social media

| Inbound Encounters | Customers seeking assistance or support from the service provider | Phone calls to customer service, email inquiries |
| Outbound Encounters | Proactive contact initiated by the service provider with customers | Follow-up calls, personalized offers, marketing |

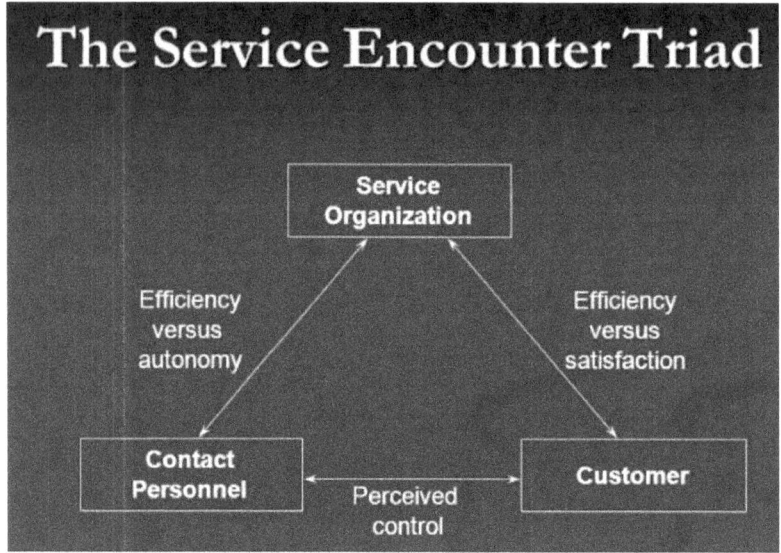

The service encounter triad

The service encounter triad, also known as the "service triangle" or "service marketing triangle," is a conceptual framework that highlights the dynamic relationship between three key elements involved in a service encounter. These elements include the customer, the service provider (frontline employee), and the organization (the company). The triad illustrates how the interactions and relationships among these three parties shape the overall service experience and customer satisfaction.

1. Customer: The customer is at the center of the service encounter triad. They are the recipient of the service and play a crucial role in shaping their own

service experience. The customer's expectations, perceptions, needs, and behaviors influence how they evaluate the service quality.

2. Service Provider (Frontline Employee): The frontline employee represents the service provider and is directly involved in delivering the service to the customer. They are the face of the organization and have a significant impact on the customer's experience. The employee's attitude, competence, and communication skills can influence customer satisfaction and loyalty.

3. Organization (Company): The organization represents the company or service provider as a whole. It sets the service standards, policies, and processes that guide frontline employees in delivering services. The organization's culture, support systems, and resources all play a role in shaping the customer experience.

Key Points of the Service Encounter Triad:

1. Interdependency: The three elements in the service encounter triad are interdependent, meaning they are interconnected and affect one another. The customer's perception of the service is influenced by both the frontline employee's behavior and the organization's policies and practices.

2. Customer-Centric Focus: Placing the customer at the center of the triad emphasizes the importance of understanding and meeting customer needs and expectations. A customer-centric approach is critical for delivering exceptional service experiences.

3. Employee Empowerment: Empowering frontline employees with the necessary skills, authority, and support is vital for creating positive service encounters. Engaged and empowered employees are

more likely to deliver quality service and satisfy customer needs.

4. Service Design and Management: Organizations must design service processes and systems that support frontline employees in delivering quality service. Effective service management ensures that employees have the resources and training needed to meet customer expectations.

5. Continuous Improvement: The service encounter triad encourages continuous improvement efforts to enhance the customer experience. Organizations should actively seek customer feedback, measure service performance, and make necessary adjustments based on insights gained.

Service Organization, Contact Personnel, The Customer

Service Organization: The service organization is the core entity responsible for providing services to its customers. It encompasses the entire infrastructure, management, and resources required to deliver the services offered. This entity establishes the overarching service strategy and vision, which guides the organization's service delivery approach.

Key roles of the service organization:

- Defining Service Offerings: The service organization determines the range of services it will provide to its target market. It identifies the unique value proposition and benefits that distinguish its services from competitors.

- Setting Service Standards: To ensure consistent and high-quality service delivery, the service organization sets service standards and performance benchmarks. These standards outline the expectations for service quality, customer interactions, and service efficiency.

- Creating Service Processes: The organization designs and implements service processes that govern how services are delivered. These processes may involve steps for customer onboarding, service execution, and follow-up support.

- Establishing Policies and Guidelines: The service organization develops policies and guidelines to govern service-related decisions, such as handling customer complaints, refund procedures, and service warranties.

- Training and Support: The organization provides training and ongoing support to contact personnel to equip them with the necessary skills, product knowledge, and tools to deliver excellent service.

- Monitoring and Measuring Performance: The service organization continuously monitors service performance, customer satisfaction, and feedback to identify areas for improvement and measure progress towards service goals.

Contact Personnel (Frontline Employees): Contact personnel, often referred to as frontline employees, are the face of the service organization to the customer. They directly interact with customers during the service encounter, and their behavior, competence, and attitude significantly impact the customer experience.

Key roles of contact personnel:

- Customer Interaction: Frontline employees engage with customers directly, whether in-person, over the phone, or through digital channels. They greet customers, listen to their needs, and provide assistance.

- Service Delivery: Contact personnel are responsible for delivering the actual service as per the organization's standards. They perform tasks, handle inquiries, and ensure a smooth service process.

- Customer Relationship Building: Frontline employees build rapport with customers and strive to create positive relationships. They aim to establish trust and loyalty through personalized interactions.

- Problem Resolution: Contact personnel handle customer complaints and issues, seeking solutions and ensuring customer satisfaction. Effective service recovery can turn a negative experience into a positive one.

- Communication: Frontline employees communicate service-related information, product details, and promotions to customers, ensuring they are well-informed.

- Upselling and Cross-selling: In certain situations, contact personnel may identify opportunities to upsell or cross-sell additional services or products to customers, enhancing revenue generation for the organization.

The Customer: The customer is the focal point of the service encounter and plays a central role in the entire service delivery process. Customers seek services to fulfill specific needs, solve problems, or gain value from the service provider.

Key aspects of the customer's role:

- Identifying Needs and Expectations: Customers determine their specific needs and expectations when seeking a service. They may have different preferences, priorities, and desired outcomes.

- Evaluating Service Quality: The customer evaluates the quality of the service experience based on how well the service organization and contact personnel meet their expectations. Positive service encounters lead to customer satisfaction.

- Providing Feedback: Customers provide feedback on their experiences with the service. This feedback is valuable for the service organization to understand areas of improvement and identify opportunities for enhancing the service offering.

- Decision-Making: Customers make decisions regarding whether to continue using the service, make repeat purchases, or recommend the service to others based on their overall satisfaction and perception of value.

- Influence on Others: Satisfied customers become brand advocates and may influence potential customers through positive word-of-mouth recommendations.

Creating Customer Service Orientation

Creating a customer service orientation within an organization involves fostering a culture where all employees are dedicated to meeting customer needs and providing exceptional service experiences. Here are some key steps to establish a customer service-oriented culture:

1. Define a Customer-Centric Vision: Establish a clear and inspiring vision that puts the customer at the center of everything the organization does. Ensure

that this vision is communicated and understood at all levels of the company.

2. Leadership Commitment: Leadership plays a vital role in driving a customer service orientation. Top management should demonstrate a genuine commitment to customer service and lead by example.

3. Employee Training and Development: Provide comprehensive training to all employees on customer service principles, communication skills, and conflict resolution. Invest in ongoing development to continuously enhance employee capabilities.

4. Empower Frontline Employees: Empower frontline employees to make decisions and resolve customer issues independently. Give them the authority and resources needed to deliver exceptional service.

5. Listen to Customer Feedback: Actively seek and listen to customer feedback through surveys, focus groups, and direct communication. Use this feedback to identify areas for improvement and to understand customer needs better.

6. Recognize and Reward Customer-Centric Behavior: Implement recognition and reward programs to acknowledge employees who consistently demonstrate a customer service mindset. Celebrate customer service success stories within the organization.

7. Develop Service Standards: Establish clear service standards and guidelines that outline the desired level of service quality. These standards should cover all customer touchpoints and interactions.

8. Service Recovery Process: Develop a robust service

recovery process to handle customer complaints and issues effectively. Turning a negative experience into a positive one can strengthen customer loyalty.

9. Benchmark and Learn from Best Practices: Benchmark against industry leaders and seek inspiration from organizations known for their exceptional customer service. Adapt and apply best practices to your unique context.

10. Celebrate Customer Success Stories: Share positive customer feedback and success stories across the organization to inspire and reinforce a customer-centric mindset.

Service Profit Chain

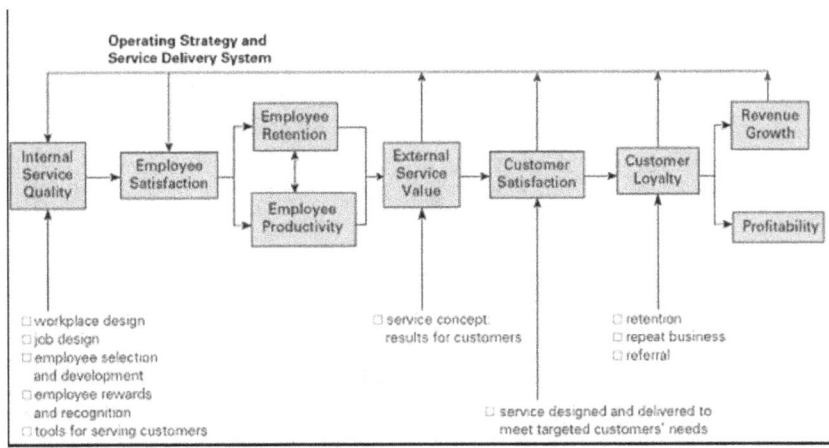

The Service Profit Chain is a business model that emphasizes the strong relationship between employee satisfaction, customer loyalty, and financial performance in service-based organizations. It was first introduced by James L. Heskett, W.

Earl Sasser, and Leonard A. Schlesinger in their book "The Service Profit Chain: How Leading Companies Link Profit and Growth to Loyalty, Satisfaction, and Value."

The model proposes that a series of interconnected factors contribute to a chain reaction that leads to increased profitability and business success. The links in the Service Profit Chain are as follows:

1. Internal Service Quality: It starts with the satisfaction and engagement of employees, commonly referred to as internal customers. When employees are satisfied, feel valued, and are equipped with the necessary tools and training, they are more likely to deliver high-quality service to external customers.

2. Satisfied and Engaged Employees: Satisfied employees are more likely to be engaged and motivated to go the extra mile in serving customers. Engaged employees have higher levels of job satisfaction, which leads to increased productivity and reduced turnover.

3. High-Quality Service Delivery: When employees are motivated and satisfied, they are more likely to deliver high-quality service to external customers. This leads to improved customer satisfaction, loyalty, and retention.

4. Customer Satisfaction: Satisfied customers are more likely to become loyal customers and repeat buyers. They are also more inclined to recommend the company to others, leading to positive word-of-mouth marketing.

5. Customer Loyalty: Loyal customers tend to be more forgiving of occasional service failures and are less likely to switch to competitors. They have a higher lifetime value, leading to increased revenue and

profitability over time.

6. Financial Performance: The chain culminates in improved financial performance for the organization. Increased customer loyalty and repeat business, coupled with reduced employee turnover, lead to higher revenues and cost savings, ultimately resulting in higher profitability.

Key principles of the Service Profit Chain:

1. Employee-Customer Linkage: The model emphasizes the direct link between employee satisfaction and customer satisfaction. Satisfied and engaged employees are more likely to deliver exceptional service, leading to higher customer satisfaction.

2. Long-Term Focus: The Service Profit Chain emphasizes the long-term view, highlighting that investing in employees and customer relationships can yield sustainable financial gains over time.

3. Employee Development: Developing employees' skills, providing training, and creating a positive work environment are critical for fostering employee satisfaction and engagement.

4. Customer-Centric Approach: The model underscores the importance of understanding and meeting customer needs to build loyalty and retention.

5. Measurement and Analysis: Measuring and analyzing key metrics, such as employee satisfaction, customer satisfaction, and financial performance, are essential for identifying areas for improvement and tracking progress over time.

By focusing on the interplay between employee satisfaction, customer loyalty, and financial performance, organizations can use the Service Profit Chain model as a strategic framework to enhance their competitive advantage, profitability, and sustainable growth in the service industry.

CHAPTER 4

Service Facility Planning:

Service Facility Planning is the process of strategically designing and organizing the physical environment in which a service will be delivered. It involves careful consideration of various factors to ensure the facility is efficient, effective, and capable of meeting customer needs and expectations. Service facility planning applies to a wide range of service industries, including healthcare, hospitality, retail, banking, transportation, and more.

Key considerations in Service Facility Planning:

1. Location: Choosing the right location for a service facility is crucial. Factors such as accessibility, visibility, proximity to target customers, and competitive analysis are taken into account. The goal is to make it convenient and attractive for customers to access the service.

2. Facility Size and Layout: Determining the appropriate size and layout of the facility depends on the specific requirements of the service. The layout should optimize the use of available space, minimize customer wait times, and streamline service processes. In a hospital, for instance, departments might be organized logically to improve patient flow.

3. Capacity Planning: Estimating the capacity needed to meet customer demand is essential to avoid long waiting times or overcrowding. Capacity planning involves forecasting demand patterns and ensuring that the facility can handle peak periods efficiently.

4. Customer Flow and Queuing: Analyzing customer

flow and queuing patterns helps to design service areas, waiting rooms, and queues effectively. Techniques like line management, digital ticketing, and self-check-in kiosks can be used to reduce customer wait times.

5. Technology Integration: The integration of technology can improve the efficiency of service delivery. For example, using online appointment systems, self-service kiosks, or mobile apps can enhance the customer experience and reduce operational costs.

6. Safety and Accessibility: Ensuring the safety and accessibility of the facility for all customers is of utmost importance. Compliance with building codes, ADA regulations, and other safety standards must be considered during the planning process.

7. Aesthetics and Atmosphere: The ambiance and aesthetics of the facility influence the customer's perception of the service. A visually appealing and well-maintained environment can create a positive impression and enhance customer satisfaction.

8. Flexibility and Adaptability: Service facility planning should account for future growth and changes in customer preferences. The facility design should be adaptable to accommodate new services or modifications in the service delivery process.

9. Cost and Budgeting: The financial aspect of service facility planning is crucial. It involves estimating costs, budgeting for construction or renovation, and ensuring that the investment aligns with the expected returns and long-term business goals.

10. Environmental Sustainability: Increasingly, service providers are incorporating environmentally sustainable practices into their facility planning.

This includes energy-efficient systems, waste reduction, and eco-friendly materials.

Servicescapes

The servicescape includes the appearance, equipment, signage and layout of a service outlet.

Service Facility Planning, specifically the concept of "Servicescapes," refers to the strategic design and management of the physical environment in which a service is delivered. The term was coined by Mary Jo Bitner in 1992 and encompasses various elements, such as layout, design, ambiance, and other tangible aspects that influence the customer's perception and experience of the service.

A Basic Environmental Psychology Model

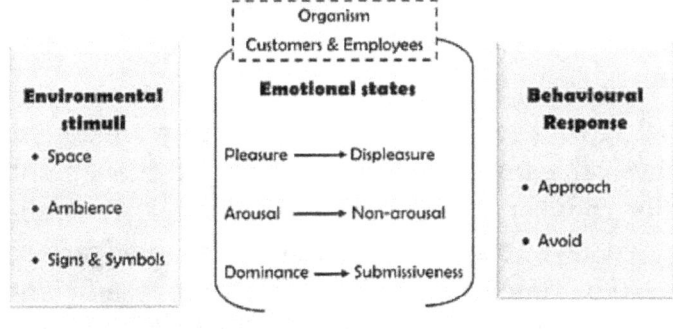

Servicescapes play a crucial role in shaping customer perceptions and behavior. A well-designed servicescape can enhance customer satisfaction, increase service usage, and foster customer loyalty. On the other hand, a poorly designed or maintained servicescape can lead to customer dissatisfaction and a negative impact on the service provider's reputation.

Key Elements of Servicescapes:

Servicescapes Model

1. **Ambient Conditions:** This refers to the background characteristics that set the tone for the service environment. It includes elements like lighting, temperature, noise levels, scent, and music. For example, a fine-dining restaurant would have soft lighting, pleasant background music, and a controlled noise level to create a relaxed and comfortable ambiance.

2. **Spatial Layout and Functionality:** The arrangement of physical elements and the flow of movement within the service facility are critical. A well-designed layout should facilitate easy navigation, reduce customer confusion, and ensure efficient service delivery. For instance, a hospital should have clear signage and easy-to-follow pathways to guide patients to different departments.

3. **Signs, Symbols, and Artifacts:** These visual cues

communicate information and create a certain atmosphere. Logos, signs, posters, and decorative elements contribute to the overall theme and branding of the service. In a retail store, strategically placed signs can guide customers to different sections or promote special offers.

4. Interior Design and Decor: The interior design, including colors, materials, furniture, and overall aesthetics, influences the emotional response of customers. Different colors evoke different emotions, and the choice of materials can convey a sense of luxury or simplicity. A spa, for example, would have calming colors and comfortable furnishings to promote relaxation.

5. Social Dimensions: The presence and behavior of other customers and employees influence the perception of the service environment. Crowded waiting areas or interactions with friendly staff can impact the overall service experience. Retailers often use trained staff to engage customers and create a positive social atmosphere.

Importance of Servicescapes:

1. Differentiation: In a competitive market, servicescapes can serve as a unique selling point for a service provider. A distinctive and attractive physical environment can set a business apart from its competitors and attract more customers.

2. Customer Experience: Servicescapes significantly influence how customers perceive the service and how they feel during their interactions. A well-designed environment can evoke positive emotions, leading to increased satisfaction and repeat business.

3. Branding: The physical environment reflects a service provider's brand image and values.

Consistency in design and branding elements reinforces the brand identity and helps in brand recall.

4. Employee Morale and Performance: An appealing and well-organized servicescape can positively impact employee morale and job satisfaction. Happy employees are more likely to deliver better customer service.

5. Service Efficiency: Proper facility planning can improve service efficiency by optimizing traffic flow, reducing waiting times, and enhancing service delivery processes.

6. Psychological Impact: Servicescapes can influence customers' perceptions of service quality and credibility. A visually appealing and well-maintained environment creates a positive impression of the service provider's competence and professionalism.

Service facility planning, with a focus on creating effective servicescapes, is an essential aspect of service management. It requires a deep understanding of customer needs and preferences, as well as consideration of the service provider's brand identity and business objectives. By carefully designing and managing the physical environment, service providers can create memorable and positive customer experiences, ultimately leading to improved customer satisfaction and loyalty.

Facility Design

Service design is the activity of planning and arranging people, infrastructure, communication and material components of a service in order to improve its quality, and the interaction between the service provider and its users. Service design may function as a way to inform changes to an existing service or create a new service entirely.

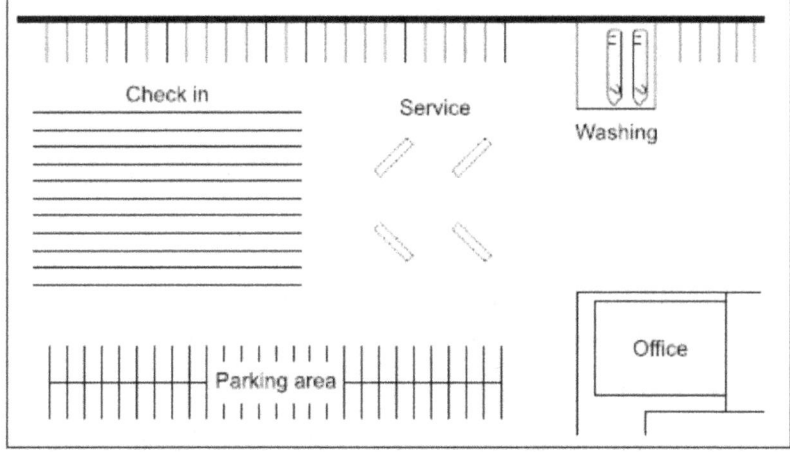

Fig. 2.12 *Service layout for car servicing*

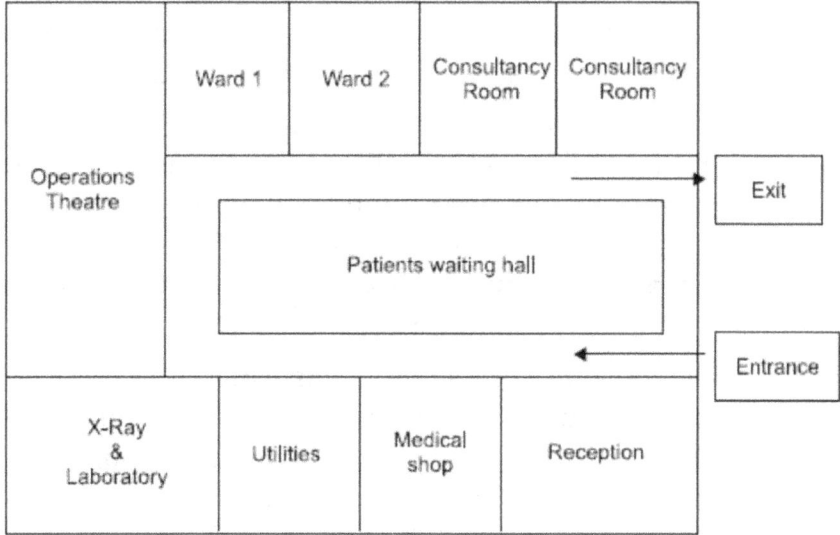

Considerations in facility design:

1. Customer Experience: The primary goal of facility design is to create a positive and memorable customer experience. The design should align with the brand image and values of the service provider, making customers feel comfortable, engaged, and satisfied during their interactions.

2. Service Process Efficiency: The layout and design

of the facility should support the smooth flow of service processes. By optimizing the arrangement of service areas, equipment, and staff workstations, service providers can minimize customer waiting times and enhance service delivery speed.

3. Spatial Planning: Facility design involves determining the appropriate allocation of space for different service areas. Analyzing customer flow, queuing patterns, and peak service demand helps in creating an efficient spatial arrangement.

4. Technology Integration: Incorporating technology into facility design can streamline service processes and enhance the overall customer experience. Examples include self-service kiosks, digital signage, mobile applications, and online reservation systems.

5. Flexibility and Adaptability: Service facilities should be designed with flexibility in mind to accommodate changes in service offerings, customer preferences, and business growth. Adaptable designs can save costs in the long term and ensure that the facility remains relevant over time.

6. Safety and Accessibility: Ensuring the safety and accessibility of the facility for all customers, including those with disabilities, is a fundamental aspect of facility design. Compliance with building codes and accessibility regulations is essential.

7. Aesthetics and Ambiance: The design should create a visually appealing environment that complements the service theme and supports the desired customer experience. The use of colors, lighting, furniture, and decor can contribute to the ambiance and emotional response of customers.

8. Employee Experience: Facility design should also consider the well-being of employees. Comfortable

workspaces, break areas, and ergonomic design can enhance employee morale and productivity, leading to better service delivery.

9. Cost and Budget: Facility design decisions need to align with the available budget and expected returns on investment. Careful cost analysis and budgeting are essential to ensure that the design meets business objectives.

Lawrence et al propose six service design principles:

1. **Human-centred**: Consider the experience of all the people affected by the service.

2. **Collaborative**: Stakeholders of various backgrounds and functions should be actively engaged in the service design process.

3. **Iterative**: Service design is an exploratory, adaptive, and experimental approach, iterating toward implementation.

4. **Sequential**: The service should be visualized and orchestrated as a sequence of interrelated actions.

5. **Real**: Needs should be researched in reality, ideas prototyped in reality, and intangible values evidenced as physical or digital reality.

6. **Holistic**: Services should sustainably address the needs of all stakeholders through the entire service and across the business

Examples of facility design in different industries:

- Healthcare: In hospitals and clinics, facility design focuses on patient flow, infection control, comfort for patients and visitors, and creating a calming atmosphere to reduce anxiety.

- Hospitality: In hotels and resorts, facility design emphasizes aesthetics, luxurious amenities, efficient check-in and check-out processes, and well-designed common areas.

- Retail: In retail stores, facility design includes store layout, product displays, and the use of technology for interactive experiences and efficient checkout processes.

- Transportation: In airports, train stations, and bus terminals, facility design aims to provide easy navigation, waiting areas, and amenities for travelers.

- Restaurants: Facility design in restaurants involves creating a pleasant dining atmosphere, efficient kitchen layout, and comfortable seating arrangements

Facility Layout

Facility Layout refers to the arrangement of various service-related components and resources to optimize the delivery of services and enhance customer experience. The primary objective is to ensure smooth operations, minimize wait times, and maximize efficiency.

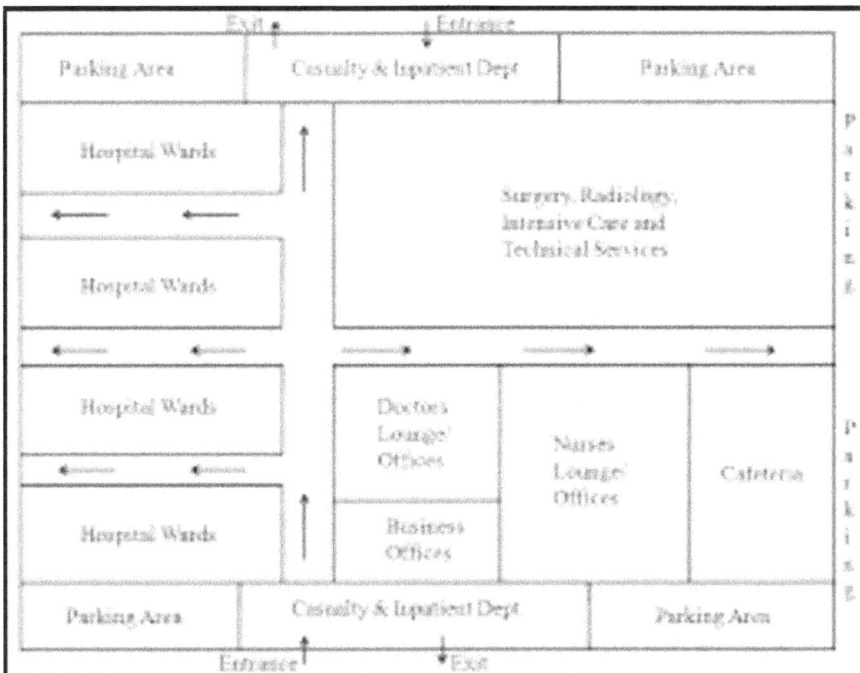

Different types of services may require different facility layouts, but here are some common examples:

1. **Retail Stores:** In a retail store, the layout is crucial for creating an inviting and easy-to-navigate environment for customers. Strategic placement of shelves, aisles, and displays can encourage product exploration and increase sales. Retailers often use grid, loop, or free-flow layouts, depending on the store's size and product assortment.

2. **Hotels:** Facility layout in hotels is essential for creating a positive guest experience. It involves organizing reception areas, guest rooms, restaurants, and amenities to ensure convenience and comfort. Hotels may use a combination of open spaces, corridors, and well-marked signage to guide guests efficiently.

3. **Hospitals:** Hospital facility layout is critical for

optimizing patient flow, minimizing wait times, and ensuring accessibility to various departments and medical facilities. Well-designed hospital layouts can enhance patient care and staff efficiency.

4. **Banks:** In banks and other financial institutions, facility layout aims to create a secure and efficient environment for customers and staff. It involves organizing teller stations, customer service areas, and private offices while considering security and privacy aspects.

5. **Restaurants:** Restaurants need a layout that facilitates efficient movement of staff and easy access for customers. The placement of kitchen areas, dining tables, and service stations is carefully considered to optimize workflow and customer satisfaction.

6. **Call Centers:** In call centers, facility layout plays a role in creating a conducive environment for customer service representatives to work efficiently. Proper workstation arrangement, breakout areas, and support facilities are taken into account.

The principles of facility layout in services focus on creating a comfortable and efficient environment for both customers and employees. It considers factors like traffic flow, space utilization, safety, accessibility, and aesthetics to achieve the desired outcomes. Additionally, advancements in technology have influenced facility layouts in services, allowing for greater integration of digital elements to enhance the customer experience.

Office Layout

Office layout is an arrangement of departments, people or workers and their equipment so as to maximize the flow of information among people, effectively utilize the space and maximize employee or worker productivity.

The decision factors for office layout are given below.

1. Smooth flow of work The office layout can be a straight line, circle or U-shaped to ensure steady & unhindered flow of work. The floor space should be free from partitions and columns.

2. Space Utilization and Uniformity: Office layout should make fullest utilization of space. Proper aisles should be provided. The furniture and other equipment's should be of uniform size and appearance with greater flexibility.

3. Working environment: Office layout must consider comfort, safety, and ventilation and light requirements.

4. Location of departments The employees performing similar functions can be grouped together. Interrelated departments with maximum flow of people or information should be placed together. Common facilities like canteen, printing facilities, client meeting room should be easily accessible.

Retail Store Layout

The retail store layout emphasizes on maximizing the net profit per square of display space. More of the customers have exposure to the products greater the sales and hence revenues. The retail stores can have strategy of focusing only a segment of customers and accordingly plan the layout. For example, the grocery stores can place daily routine items like bread, milk and eggs at the entrance of stores so that the working couples can quickly buy the goods.

Any retail store outlet can consider two factors

1) The overall arrangement or flow pattern for the store.

2) Allocation of space within that arrangement to various products

To increase the profitability, the retail store layout can consider the following points

• To encourage impulse buying the daily necessity products can be stored far away from the clear vision of the customers. In such manner the customer will view other products also which are not in the customer's buying on the way to the necessity products.

• Sufficient aisle space should be provided for free movement of customers

• Convey the mission of the store by carefully selecting the position of the lead – off department

SERVICE FACILITY LOCATION:

Service facility location is the process of strategically determining the optimal geographical location for a service-oriented business or facility. It involves analyzing various factors to identify a site that will best serve the target market, meet customer needs, and ensure efficient service delivery. The location of a service facility can significantly impact the success and profitability of the business, as it affects accessibility, convenience, and overall customer satisfaction.

Factors to consider when determining the location for a service facility:

1. **Market Demand and Customer Base:** Analyze the target market and the distribution of your customer base. Identify areas with high demand for the services you offer. Consider factors like population density, income levels, demographics, and customer preferences.

2. **Competitor Analysis:** Assess the locations of existing competitors. Avoid direct competition by choosing a location where your service will complement rather than directly compete with

other businesses.

3. **Accessibility and Proximity:** Ensure that the facility is easily accessible to your target customers. Consider proximity to major transportation routes, public transportation hubs, and parking availability.

4. **Visibility and Signage:** Opt for a location with good visibility to attract potential customers. Well-designed signage can also enhance your facility's visibility and brand recognition.

5. **Costs and Financial Considerations:** Evaluate the costs associated with setting up and maintaining the facility at different locations. Consider factors such as rent, utilities, taxes, and labor costs.

6. **Zoning and Legal Regulations:** Ensure that the intended type of service facility is permitted by local zoning regulations. Be aware of any legal restrictions or requirements that may impact your business operations.

7. **Infrastructure and Utilities:** Check the availability and reliability of essential utilities like water, electricity, internet, and telecommunications. A robust infrastructure is crucial for smooth service delivery.

8. **Future Growth and Expansion:** Consider the potential for future growth and expansion. Choose a location that allows for scalability and accommodates increasing demand.

9. **Safety and Security:** Prioritize the safety and security of both customers and employees. Research the crime rates and safety measures in the area.

10. **Local Demographics and Culture:** Understand the local culture and how it might influence the delivery of your services. Cultural preferences and traditions

can impact the success of your business.

Service Facility Location Planning

> **Flexibility**: of a location is a measure of the degree to which the service can react to changing economic situations. Therefore, in location decisions plan for future economic changes and portfolio effect.

> **Competitive positioning**: refers to methods by which the firm can establish itself relative to its competitors. Multiple location or prime location can be barrier to entry.

> **Demand management**: it is the ability to control the quality, quantity, and timing of demand. For example, a hotel can control demand by locating near a diverse set of market generators that supply a steady demand .

> **Focus**: can be developed by offering the same narrowly defined service at many locations.

Classification of Service Facility Location Issues

Service facility location issues can be classified into various categories based on the factors and challenges involved in the decision-making process. Here are some common classifications of service facility location issues:

1. **Market-Related Issues:**

    - Market Demand: Understanding the level of demand for the services in different locations and identifying areas with a high concentration of potential customers.

    - Customer Profile: Analyzing the demographics, preferences, and behavior of the target customer base in various locations.

    - Competitor Presence: Assessing the competition in different areas and identifying opportunities to differentiate the services.

2. **Economic and Financial Issues:**

- Operating Costs: Evaluating the costs associated with setting up and running the service facility in different locations, including rent, utilities, labor, and taxes.

- Return on Investment (ROI): Determining the potential profitability of the service facility in each location and comparing the expected returns.

3. **Geographical and Infrastructure Factors:**

- Accessibility: Assessing the ease of access to the facility for customers, suppliers, and employees, considering transportation routes and connectivity.

- Infrastructure Availability: Analyzing the availability and reliability of essential utilities and services such as water, electricity, internet, and telecommunications.

4. **Regulatory and Legal Considerations:**

- Zoning and Permits: Understanding local zoning regulations and obtaining the necessary permits and approvals for setting up the service facility.

- Compliance: Ensuring the facility location complies with environmental, safety, and other legal requirements.

5. **Risk Assessment:**

- Business Risks: Identifying potential risks and challenges associated with specific locations, such as economic instability, natural disasters, or security concerns.

- Environmental Risks: Considering environmental factors like flooding, seismic activity, or pollution that may impact the facility's operations.

6. **Cultural and Social Factors:**

- Cultural Fit: Assessing the compatibility of the service with the cultural preferences and practices of the local population.

- Social Impact: Understanding how the facility's presence may affect the community and vice versa.

Facility Location Technique-Single and Multiple Facilities

Facility location techniques are methods used to determine the optimal location(s) for a facility or facilities, considering various factors such as costs, demand, transportation, and other relevant parameters. There are different techniques available for both single and multiple facilities, and they help businesses make informed decisions regarding their facility location strategies.

Single Facility Location Techniques:

1. **Factor Rating Method:** In this technique, different factors influencing the facility location, such as labor availability, transportation costs, proximity to raw materials, market demand, etc., are assigned weights based on their importance. Potential locations are then rated and scored based on these factors, and the one with the highest overall score is considered the best location.

2. **The Center of Gravity Method:** This method is suitable when demand points have different weights or volumes. It involves calculating the

weighted geographic center of the demand points to find the most centralized location that minimizes transportation costs.

3. **Load-Distance Technique:** This technique aims to minimize transportation costs by locating the facility closer to the demand points that generate more business. It calculates the total load and distance for each potential location, and the one with the lowest total is chosen.

4. **Break-Even Analysis:** This method compares the total costs at different potential locations and identifies the point at which costs will be the same for all locations. It helps in determining the range of demand volumes for which a particular location is most cost-effective.

Multiple Facility Location Techniques:

1. **Optimal Location of Facilities (OLF):** This technique involves optimizing the locations of multiple facilities to minimize the overall cost of transportation, production, and distribution. It considers the demand, supply, and costs for each facility and determines the best configuration.

2. **Location-Allocation Models:** Location-allocation models are mathematical optimization models that simultaneously determine the number and location of facilities to serve specific demand points while minimizing overall costs.

3. **Maximal Covering Location Problem (MCLP):** This technique aims to maximize the coverage of service for demand points while locating a limited number of facilities. It is commonly used in the healthcare sector to determine the locations of hospitals or clinics.

4. **P-median Problem:** The P-median problem is a type of facility location model that aims to locate P facilities to minimize the average distance between facilities and demand points.

Site Considerations

When considering the site for a facility location, businesses need to take into account a wide range of factors to ensure the success and efficiency of their operations. Site considerations play a crucial role in determining the suitability of a location for a facility. Here are some key site considerations to keep in mind:

1. **Accessibility:** The site should be easily accessible to customers, suppliers, and employees. Proximity to major transportation routes (such as highways, railways, and airports) is essential for smooth logistics and supply chain operations.

2. **Demographics and Customer Base:** Analyze the demographics of the surrounding area to ensure that the site aligns with the target customer base. Consider factors such as population density, income levels, age groups, and consumer preferences.

3. **Market Demand:** Determine the level of demand for the facility's products or services in the selected area. Look for locations with a sufficient and sustainable market demand to support the business's growth.

4. **Competition:** Evaluate the presence of competitors in the area. Consider whether the market is already saturated with similar businesses or if there is an opportunity to fill a gap in the market.

5. **Zoning and Legal Regulations:** Check local zoning regulations and ensure that the chosen site is

appropriate for the intended use of the facility. Obtain any necessary permits and approvals from relevant authorities.

6. **Infrastructure and Utilities:** Assess the availability and reliability of essential infrastructure and utilities, such as water, electricity, internet connectivity, sewage systems, and waste disposal.

7. **Costs:** Consider the costs associated with acquiring the site, as well as ongoing operational costs. Evaluate factors such as land prices, rent, property taxes, and utility expenses.

8. **Environmental Factors:** Investigate any potential environmental risks or concerns associated with the site, such as pollution, flooding, or natural hazards. Ensure compliance with environmental regulations.

9. **Labor Availability:** Evaluate the availability of a skilled and suitable workforce in the vicinity of the site. Consider factors such as labor pool size, skill levels, and wage expectations.

10. **Future Growth and Expansion:** Think about the potential for future growth and expansion. Ensure that the site can accommodate the business's long-term needs and plans for scalability.

11. **Security and Safety:** Prioritize the safety and security of both employees and customers. Consider crime rates and implement necessary security measures.

12. **Proximity to Suppliers and Resources:** For manufacturing facilities, consider the proximity to suppliers, raw materials, and other resources required for production.

CHAPTER 5

Managing Service Operations

Managing service operations involves overseeing the processes, resources, and activities required to deliver high-quality services to customers. Whether in a company, organization, or any service-oriented business, effective management of service operations is essential to ensure customer satisfaction, operational efficiency, and overall success.

Aspects of managing service operations:

1. Service Design: Begin by designing the service offerings based on customer needs and preferences. This includes identifying the target market, understanding customer expectations, and creating service packages that meet those requirements.

2. Service Strategy: Develop a clear strategy that aligns with the organization's overall goals. Determine the value proposition, pricing strategies, service level agreements (SLAs), and the positioning of your services in the market.

3. Resource Management: Ensure you have the right resources, including skilled staff, equipment, technology, and materials, to deliver services effectively and efficiently. Optimize resource allocation to meet demand fluctuations and avoid over or underutilization.

4. Process Optimization: Streamline service delivery processes to minimize delays, reduce errors, and enhance the overall customer experience. Use tools like Lean or Six Sigma to identify bottlenecks and inefficiencies.

5. Service Quality Management: Implement systems to monitor and maintain service quality. This includes customer feedback mechanisms, service level monitoring, and continuous improvement initiatives to address issues and enhance service performance.

6. Service Metrics and KPIs: Define key performance indicators (KPIs) that measure the success of service operations. Metrics such as response time, customer satisfaction scores, and first-time resolution rates can help track performance and identify areas for improvement.

7. Staff Training and Development: Invest in training programs to ensure that your employees have the necessary skills and knowledge to deliver services effectively. Continuous learning and skill development are crucial in service-oriented industries.

8. Technology Integration: Leverage technology to enhance service delivery. This can involve using customer relationship management (CRM) systems, ticketing platforms, automation tools, and data analytics to better understand customer needs and optimize processes.

9. Incident and Problem Management: Develop a robust incident and problem management process to address service disruptions promptly and find root causes to prevent future occurrences.

10. Continuous Improvement: Emphasize a culture of continuous improvement, where employees are encouraged to identify areas for enhancement and innovation in service delivery.

11. Customer Relationship Management: Build strong

relationships with customers through personalized communication, addressing their concerns promptly, and going the extra mile to exceed expectations.

12. Risk Management: Identify potential risks that could impact service operations and implement strategies to mitigate those risks effectively.

Forecasting demand for services

Forecasting demand for services is a crucial aspect of service operations management, as it helps businesses and organizations prepare for future customer needs, allocate resources efficiently, and maintain high levels of customer satisfaction.

Methods to forecast demand for services:

1. Historical Data Analysis: Start by analyzing historical data on service demand, including customer volumes, patterns, and trends. This data provides valuable insights into seasonal variations, growth rates, and any recurring patterns that can be used as a basis for forecasting.

2. Market Research and Customer Surveys: Conduct market research and customer surveys to gather information on customer preferences, expectations, and potential changes in demand. Feedback from customers and prospects can help refine your forecasts and adapt to changing market conditions.

3. Time Series Analysis: Utilize time series analysis techniques to identify patterns in historical data and project them into the future. Time series forecasting methods, such as moving averages, exponential smoothing, and autoregressive integrated moving average (ARIMA) models, can be useful in predicting

demand patterns.

4. Trend Analysis: Identify long-term trends in the market or industry that might affect service demand. For example, changes in demographics, technological advancements, or economic factors can have significant impacts on demand.

5. Seasonality Analysis: Take into account any seasonal variations in service demand. Seasonality refers to regular patterns that occur during specific periods, such as holidays, festivals, or certain times of the year.

6. Leading Indicators: Identify leading indicators or factors that correlate with changes in service demand. These indicators can provide early signals of potential shifts in demand.

7. Customer Behavior Analysis: Analyze customer behavior data to understand how different customer segments utilize services and how their preferences might change over time.

8. Collaboration with Sales and Marketing Teams: Collaborate closely with sales and marketing teams to gather insights into upcoming promotions, advertising campaigns, or new product launches that may impact service demand.

9. Scenario Planning: Develop multiple scenarios based on different assumptions and potential market conditions. This helps in building flexibility into your forecasts and better prepares your organization for various outcomes.

10. Use of Technology and Data Analytics: Leverage advanced technologies and data analytics tools to process large amounts of data quickly and gain deeper insights into demand patterns and trends.

11. Cross-Functional Input: Involve key stakeholders from various departments in the forecasting process to gain diverse perspectives and align the forecast with business objectives.

12. Continuous Review and Improvement: Regularly review the accuracy of your forecasts and adjust your forecasting methods as needed. Demand forecasting is an ongoing process that requires continuous improvement.

Forecasting Demand

- Subjective Models
  - Delphi Method
  - Cross-Impact
  - Historical Analogy

- Causal Models
  - Regression Models
  - Econometric Models

- Time Series Models
  - N-Period Moving Average
  - Simple Exponential Smoothing
  - Exponential Smoothing with Trend or Seasonal Adjustment

Subjective models:

Subjective models, also known as qualitative or judgmental models, are a type of forecasting method that relies on human judgment, experience, and expertise rather than statistical or quantitative data. In these models, forecasters make predictions based on their intuition, knowledge of the industry, and insights into market dynamics. Subjective forecasting can be especially useful when historical data is limited, unavailable, or when there are significant changes or uncertainties in the environment that cannot be captured by traditional quantitative methods.

Subjective forecasting models:

1. Expert Opinion: Subjective models often involve gathering opinions and insights from subject matter experts within the organization or industry. These experts provide their predictions based on their expertise, experience, and understanding of the market.

2. Delphi Method: The Delphi method is a specific type of subjective forecasting that involves gathering opinions from a panel of experts in multiple rounds. The experts' responses are anonymized and aggregated between rounds, and the process continues until a consensus or convergence of opinions is achieved.

3. Scenario Planning: Subjective forecasting can involve creating various scenarios based on different assumptions and potential future developments. These scenarios help organizations plan for multiple possible outcomes and develop contingency strategies.

4. Market Surveys: Surveys of customers, suppliers, or industry stakeholders can provide valuable qualitative data for subjective forecasting. These surveys collect opinions on potential future trends, market demands, and changes in consumer preferences.

5. Focus Groups: Focus groups are used to gain qualitative insights from a selected group of customers or potential users of a service. The discussions in focus groups can provide valuable information on perceptions, needs, and expectations, which can be used in forecasting.

6. Management Judgment: Decision-makers and

managers within an organization may rely on their experience and intuition to make predictions about future demand, market conditions, and other relevant factors.

7. Sales Force Composite: In this approach, the sales team provides their estimates of future sales based on their interactions with customers and insights into the market.

Subjective models have both strengths and limitations. Some of the advantages include:

- Flexibility: Subjective models can be applied in situations where historical data is scarce or unreliable.

- Quick Response: These models can be quickly deployed when time is limited, and forecasts are needed urgently.

- Incorporating Soft Information: Subjective models can capture "soft" information that is not easily quantifiable, such as qualitative market trends or customer sentiments.

On the other hand, subjective models may have some drawbacks:

- Bias: Forecasts can be influenced by personal biases of the experts or forecasters, leading to potential inaccuracies.

- Lack of Quantifiability: Subjective forecasts may not provide precise numerical estimates, making it challenging to measure accuracy.

- Limited Scope: The reliance on human judgment may overlook some important factors, leading to incomplete forecasts.

Delphi Method

- Delphi Method
    - Developed at the Rand Corporation by Olaf Helmer
    - Method is based on expert opinion
    - People with expertise are asked to answer some question (no interaction among respondents)
    - Answers are grouped and the placed into quartiles based on the frequency in which they were mentioned
    - Respondents review the results and answers in the extreme quartiles must be justified.
    - Continued iterative process

The Delphi method is a structured, iterative, and anonymous forecasting technique used to gather opinions and insights from a panel of experts on a specific topic. It was developed in the 1950s by the RAND Corporation as a means to obtain reliable consensus-based forecasts from a group of knowledgeable individuals. The Delphi method is particularly useful when dealing with complex or uncertain issues, where there is limited data, or when quantitative forecasting approaches are impractical or insufficient.

Delphi method process:

1. Expert Panel Selection: A panel of experts, typically ranging from 10 to 20 individuals, is carefully selected based on their knowledge, experience, and expertise in the subject matter. These experts can be internal or external to the organization conducting the Delphi study.

2. Round-Based Iterations: The Delphi method consists of multiple rounds of surveys/questionnaires. In each round, the experts are asked to provide their forecasts, opinions, or judgments on the topic under consideration.

3. Anonymity: The process is designed to maintain anonymity, meaning that the individual responses

are not attributed to specific experts. This anonymity encourages honest and unbiased responses, reduces the influence of dominant personalities, and minimizes the risk of groupthink.

4. Feedback and Compilation: After each round, the responses are collected, summarized, and compiled by the facilitator or researchers conducting the Delphi study. The participants receive feedback on the group's aggregated responses without knowing the identities of the other experts.

5. Controlled Feedback: In subsequent rounds, the participants are encouraged to review the group's aggregated responses and potentially revise their own forecasts or judgments based on the information provided. This iterative process continues until a consensus or convergence of opinions is reached or until a predetermined number of rounds is completed.

6. Consensus Building: The Delphi method aims to achieve consensus among the experts by iteratively refining and revising their forecasts. However, achieving full consensus is not always the goal, and some level of disagreement may persist.

7. Termination Criteria: The Delphi study concludes when the responses converge to a certain degree, when a predefined level of consensus is reached, or when the number of rounds reaches a predetermined limit.

Cross Impact Analysis

- This analysis assumes that a future event is related to the occurrence of an earlier event
- If historical data shows that as gas prices go up by 50 cents a gallon, mass transit ridership increases by 100 people
- If there are deviations in this trend, experts go back and evaluate what happened

Cross-impact analysis, also known as cross-impact matrix method, is a systematic technique used to analyze the interrelationships and dependencies between different factors or variables within a complex system. It is often employed in strategic planning, scenario analysis, and futures studies to understand how changes in one variable can influence or impact other variables in the system.

The process of cross-impact analysis typically involves the following steps:

1. Identifying Factors: Begin by identifying the key factors or variables that are relevant to the system being analyzed. These factors could be internal to the organization, external environmental factors, or a combination of both.

2. Constructing a Cross-Impact Matrix: Create a matrix where each factor is listed as both the row and column headings. The cells of the matrix represent the relationships between the factors. The experts or stakeholders involved in the analysis provide their judgments on the direction and strength of the relationships.

3. Assessing Interrelationships: Experts or stakeholders evaluate how changes in one factor would affect the other factors in the matrix. They assign scores or values to indicate the magnitude and direction of the impact. Typically, the impact is scored as positive (promoting) or negative (hindering) and can range from weak to strong.

4. Weighting the Impact: Depending on the significance of each factor, weights may be assigned to indicate their relative importance. This step is optional and can be useful when some factors have a more substantial influence on the overall system than others.

5. Calculating Cumulative Impact: Calculate the cumulative impact of each factor by considering its individual impact and how it interacts with other factors in the matrix. This process helps to understand the system's complexity and the potential emergence of feedback loops or cascading effects.

6. Scenario Analysis: Use the cross-impact analysis results to explore different scenarios and understand how changes in one or more factors could lead to various outcomes. Scenarios can be used to assess risks, opportunities, and alternative strategic decisions.

The output of cross-impact analysis can be visualized as a cross-impact matrix, a network diagram, or through other graphical representations. This analysis provides valuable insights into the complex relationships between variables, helps identify critical factors that drive the system's behavior, and assists in making more informed strategic decisions.

Electricity price will increase	A		0	2	1	3	-3	0	0	-1	0
Wind and solar power production will increase considerably	B	-3		4	1	-2	-1	1	1	0	4
Electricity storage will increase considerably	C	-1	2		-1	-1	-1	0	-1	2	2
Control of electricity consumption will increase	D	1	0	3		-1	-1	0	-1	-3	0
New nuclear power plants will be constructed	E	1	-2	0	-2		2	0	0	0	-1
Electricity consumption will increase	F	2	1	1	1	2		0	2	3	1
GDP will grow considerably	G	1	2	0	0	1	2		1	0	0
Electricity transmission capacity from neighbouring countries will increase	H	-2	1	-1	-1	1	0	0		0	0
Fluctuations in electricity consumption will increase	I	1	0	2	4	0	0	0	1		1
Fluctuations in electricity production will increase	J	1	0	4	3	0	0	0	1	0	

Historical Analogy

- Where a forecast may be derived by using the history of a similar product

- Where an existing product or generic product could be used as a model.

- Example can be complementary or substitute product.

- Demand for CD is caused by DVD players.

In demand forecasting, historical analogy involves using past demand patterns and trends as a basis for predicting future demand. It relies on the assumption that historical demand behavior is likely to repeat or have some relevance in the future, making it a valuable technique when historical data is available, and the market conditions are relatively stable.

Process of historical analogy:

1. Data Collection: Gather historical data on past demand for the product or service being forecasted. This data should cover a sufficiently long period to capture different market conditions, seasonal variations, and any notable trends.

2. Pattern Identification: Analyze the historical data to identify recurring patterns, such as seasonal fluctuations, cyclical trends, or long-term growth patterns. Identifying these patterns is crucial for establishing the basis of the forecast.

3. Seasonal Adjustment: If the demand exhibits seasonal patterns, apply seasonal adjustments to smooth out the data and identify the underlying trend.

4. Trend Analysis: Analyze the historical data to identify any long-term trends or changes in demand. Trends may indicate a steady growth or decline in demand over time, which can help in making long-term forecasts.

5. Similarity Assessment: Identify periods in the historical data that are similar to the current or future forecast period in terms of market conditions, economic environment, consumer behavior, and other relevant factors.

Causal Models and time series models

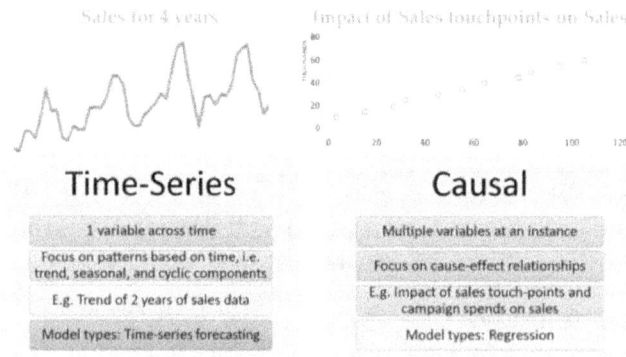

1. Causal Models:

Causal models, also known as explanatory or regression models, focus on identifying and analyzing cause-and-effect relationships between variables. These models are based on the assumption that changes in one or more independent variables cause changes in the dependent variable, which is the variable to be forecasted. Causal models are commonly used when there is a clear theoretical understanding of the relationships between variables, and when historical data is available for both the dependent and independent variables.

Key features of causal models:

- **Identify Relationships:** Causal models aim to quantify the influence of independent variables on the dependent variable through statistical relationships, often expressed as regression equations.

- **Use of External Factors:** Causal models can incorporate external factors (explanatory variables) that are believed to affect the dependent variable. For example, in demand forecasting, factors like advertising expenditure, price changes, or economic indicators could be included as independent variables.

- **Assumption of Causality:** Causal models assume that changes in independent variables cause changes in the dependent variable, and not the other way around.

- **Interpretability:** Causal models offer interpretability, as they provide insights into the direction and magnitude of the impact of each independent variable on the dependent variable.

Time series Models	Causal (Associative) Models
Assumptions	
History (in terms of the components of time series - trend, seasonality, cycles) will repeat itself	Historical relationship between "dependent" and "independent" variables will remain valid in future
	Independent variables are easy to predict
Procedures	
Collect several periods of history	Collect several periods of history on the independent and the dependent variables
Try many different methods and choose the one that minimizes a chosen measure of error	Using linear or non-linear and singular or multiple regression analysis, establish the relationship that minimizes mean squared error of forecast v/s actual
Use the method chosen to predict future	Predict the independent variable(s) first. Then using the established relationship between the independent and the dependent variables, predict the dependent variable
Data Requirement and Availability	
Detailed data by Stock Keeping units (SKUs) is necessary and often available	Aggregate data is all that is needed. However, sometimes, relevant data may not be available
Time Requirement and Availability	
Time available to do the forecasting is very short (days)	Time available to do the forecasting is usually several months
Application	
Products in the their growth or maturity phase	Products in the their growth or maturity phase
Short term forecasts	Medium term forecasts

2. Time Series Models:

Time series models are forecasting techniques that use historical data to predict future values of a variable over time. These models do not explicitly consider the relationships between variables but instead focus on identifying patterns and trends within the time series data itself.

Key features of time series models:

- **Temporal Patterns:** Time series models analyze past observations to identify patterns such as seasonality, trends, and cyclic fluctuations.

- **No External Factors:** Time series models do not involve external variables or causal relationships.

They rely solely on past values of the variable being forecasted.

- **Forecasting Horizon:** Time series models are well-suited for short- to medium-term forecasting, where the future values are predicted based on past patterns.

- **Stationarity:** Time series models often assume stationarity, meaning that statistical properties of the time series data remain constant over time.

- **Common Methods:** Common time series models include moving averages, exponential smoothing, and autoregressive integrated moving average (ARIMA) models.

Managing capacity and demand:

Managing capacity and demand is a critical aspect of operations management for any business or service-oriented organization. It involves ensuring that the organization's resources and capabilities align with the level of demand from customers or clients. Effective capacity and demand management are essential for maintaining operational efficiency, meeting customer needs, and maximizing revenue and profitability.

Strategies for managing capacity and demand:

1. Forecasting Demand: Use historical data, market research, and other relevant information to forecast future demand. Accurate demand forecasts serve as a foundation for capacity planning and resource allocation.

2. Capacity Planning: Based on demand forecasts, develop a capacity plan that outlines the resources required to meet the expected demand levels. This plan should consider factors such as labor,

equipment, facilities, and technology.

3. Flexibility in Capacity: Design your capacity to be flexible and scalable. This flexibility allows the organization to respond to changes in demand without significant disruptions or additional costs.

4. Utilization Optimization: Strive to optimize the utilization of existing capacity. Avoid underutilization, which can lead to inefficiencies, and prevent overutilization, which may result in service delays or quality issues.

5. Resource Allocation: Allocate resources efficiently based on demand patterns. This might involve adjusting staffing levels, scheduling maintenance during low-demand periods, or outsourcing during peak periods.

6. Demand Shaping: Implement marketing and pricing strategies to influence customer demand and smooth out demand peaks and valleys. For example, offer promotions during low-demand periods to encourage customers to spread their purchases over time.

7. Inventory Management: In product-based businesses, effective inventory management can help buffer fluctuations in demand. Maintain an optimal inventory level to balance customer demand with the cost of carrying inventory.

Strategies for Matching Capacity and Demand for Services

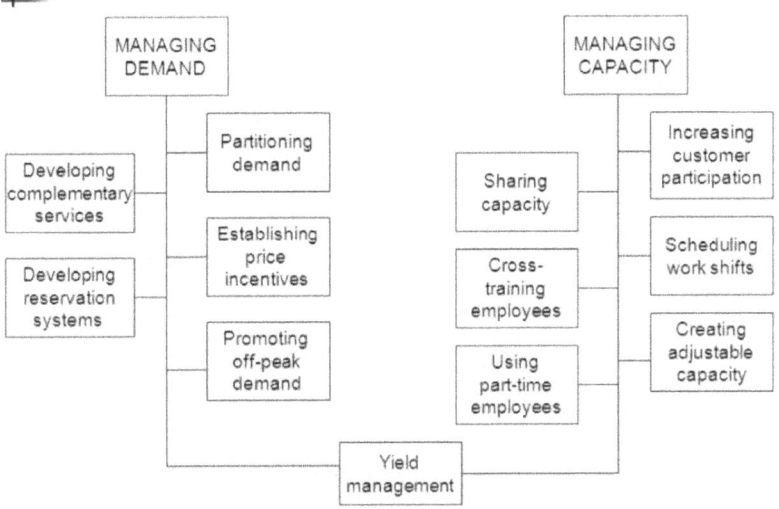

Strategies for managing demand

Managing demand effectively is crucial for businesses to ensure optimal resource utilization, maintain customer satisfaction, and enhance overall performance. Here are some strategies for managing demand:

1. Demand Forecasting: Implement a robust demand forecasting process to predict future customer demand accurately. Use historical data, market trends, and customer insights to make informed forecasts.

2. Pricing and Promotion: Adjust pricing and promotional strategies based on demand patterns. Offer discounts or promotions during low-demand periods to encourage customer purchases and balance demand across time.

3. Product and Service Bundling: Create product or service bundles to stimulate demand for less

popular items or services. Bundling can increase the perceived value for customers and lead to higher overall sales.

4. Seasonal and Time-Based Strategies: Tailor offerings and promotions to suit seasonal variations and specific times of the day, week, or year when demand is typically higher.

5. Capacity Constraints: Set capacity limits and manage demand during peak periods to avoid overloading resources. Implement reservation systems, appointment scheduling, or time-based pricing to smooth demand.

6. Waiting Line Management: Optimize waiting times for customers during peak periods by employing efficient queuing systems or offering priority services to specific customer segments.

7. Demand Shaping: Encourage customers to shift demand from peak periods to off-peak periods through incentives like off-peak pricing, loyalty programs, or early bird discounts.

8. Communication and Customer Education: Communicate transparently with customers about demand fluctuations, product availability, and potential delays. Educate customers about the benefits of using services during less busy times.

9. Inventory Management: In retail and distribution businesses, manage inventory levels to match demand fluctuations. Use just-in-time (JIT) inventory systems to reduce carrying costs and respond to real-time demand.

10. Multi-Channel Strategy: Diversify sales channels, such as physical stores, online platforms, and mobile apps, to capture a broader customer base and spread

demand across different channels.

11. Customer Segmentation: Segment customers based on their preferences, buying behavior, and price sensitivity. Tailor marketing strategies and promotions to target specific customer segments effectively.

12. Collaboration and Partnerships: Collaborate with suppliers, distributors, or complementary businesses to manage demand across the supply chain. Sharing information and resources can lead to better demand planning.

13. Agile Operations: Adopt agile and flexible operational practices that enable quick adjustments to changing demand. This approach helps businesses respond rapidly to unexpected fluctuations.

Strategies for Managing Capacity

Managing capacity effectively is essential to ensure that an organization's resources are optimally utilized while meeting customer needs and maintaining service quality. Here are some strategies for managing demand capacity:

1. Capacity Planning: Develop a comprehensive capacity plan that aligns with forecasted demand. This plan should outline the resources required, including personnel, equipment, facilities, and technology, to meet expected demand levels.

2. Scalability and Flexibility: Design capacity with scalability and flexibility in mind. Implement systems and processes that allow the organization to adjust capacity quickly in response to changing demand.

3. Peak Demand Management: Implement strategies to

manage peak demand periods. This might include offering appointment scheduling, reservation systems, or peak pricing to spread demand more evenly.

4. Demand Forecasting: Use data-driven demand forecasting techniques to anticipate fluctuations in demand accurately. Regularly review and update forecasts to align capacity planning accordingly.

5. Multi-Site Operations: Consider establishing multiple locations or facilities to distribute demand and serve different regions more effectively. Multi-site operations can also serve as backups during disruptions.

6. Cross-Training and Skill Development: Cross-train employees to perform multiple roles. This flexibility allows for better resource allocation and can help manage capacity during peak periods or staffing shortages.

7. Outsourcing and Partnerships: Collaborate with external partners or outsource certain functions to manage capacity constraints. Outsourcing can provide access to additional resources without incurring significant fixed costs.

8. Buffer Inventory: In manufacturing or distribution businesses, maintain buffer inventory to handle sudden demand spikes and ensure products are available when needed.

9. Resource Sharing: Consider resource sharing with other organizations during periods of excess capacity. This can be beneficial for industries with seasonal demand variations.

10. Continuous Monitoring: Continuously monitor actual demand and capacity utilization. Analyze

data regularly to identify potential bottlenecks or opportunities for capacity adjustments.

11. Demand Shaping: Implement demand shaping strategies to encourage customers to shift their demand to off-peak periods. This could include incentives, discounts, or loyalty programs.

12. Technology Adoption: Leverage technology to optimize capacity management. Use data analytics, automation, and AI-driven solutions to improve forecasting accuracy and resource allocation.

13. Customer Communication: Keep customers informed about capacity constraints and potential delays. Transparent communication helps manage customer expectations and prevents dissatisfaction.

14. Contingency Planning: Develop contingency plans for unexpected fluctuations in demand or disruptions in operations. Having a well-prepared plan can help minimize the impact of unforeseen events.

Yield Management

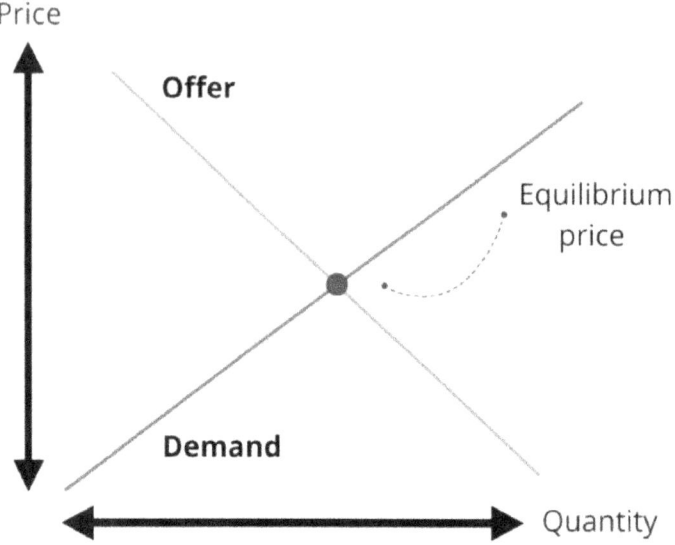

Yield management, also known as revenue management, is a pricing strategy and revenue optimization technique used by businesses to maximize revenue from available inventory or resources. It involves dynamically adjusting prices based on fluctuations in demand, capacity, and market conditions to optimize revenue and profitability. Yield management is commonly used in industries such as hospitality, airlines, rental car companies, and entertainment venues, where perishable inventory (e.g., hotel rooms, airline seats) is sold in advance.

Principles and strategies of yield management:

> 1. Demand Forecasting: Accurate demand forecasting is the foundation of yield management. Businesses

use historical data, market trends, and other relevant information to predict future demand patterns.

2. Price Discrimination: Yield management relies on price discrimination, where different prices are charged to different customer segments based on their willingness to pay. This allows businesses to capture more revenue from customers willing to pay higher prices.

3. Variable Pricing: Prices are not fixed but are adjusted based on demand and other factors. During periods of high demand, prices are increased, while during low demand, prices may be discounted to stimulate sales.

4. Segmentation: Customer segmentation is crucial in yield management. Customers are grouped based on factors such as booking time, length of stay, and purchase behavior. This segmentation helps in tailoring pricing strategies to specific customer groups.

5. Time-Based Pricing: Prices may vary based on the time of booking or usage. Early booking, last-minute reservations, or specific time slots may have different price points.

6. Capacity Management: Yield management focuses on optimizing capacity utilization. By adjusting prices, businesses can fill available capacity more effectively and avoid overbooking.

7. Overbooking and No-Show Management: In industries prone to no-shows (e.g., hotels, airlines), overbooking is used strategically to ensure full capacity even if some customers do not show up.

8. Continuous Monitoring and Adjustment: Yield management is an ongoing process. Prices and

inventory availability are continually monitored, and adjustments are made in real-time to respond to changing market conditions.

9. Upselling and Cross-Selling: Yield management strategies may include offering upsells or cross-sells to customers to enhance their experience and increase revenue.

10. Forecasting and Optimization Tools: Advanced software and analytics tools are often employed to assist in demand forecasting, price optimization, and decision-making.

CHAPTER 6

MANAGING WAITING LINES

The waiting line or queue management is a critical part of service industry. It deals with issue of treatment of customers in sense reduce wait time and improvement of service.

A waiting line, also known as a queue, is a common phenomenon that occurs when customers or entities wait in line for service or processing. Waiting lines can be found in various settings, including retail stores, banks, airports, restaurants, call centers, healthcare facilities, and transportation services.

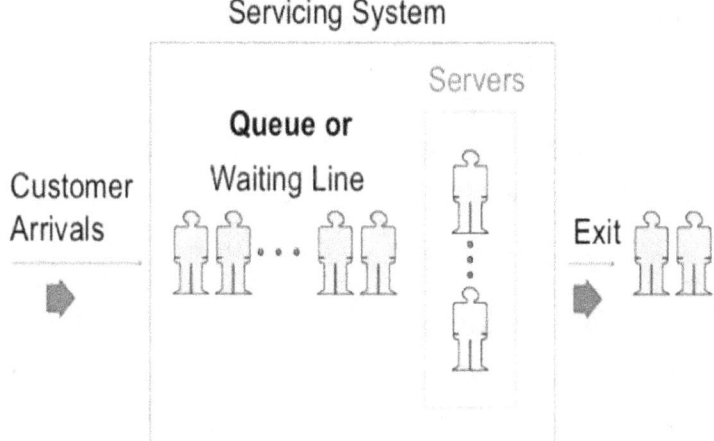

Key characteristics of waiting lines include:

1. Arrival Process: Customers or entities arrive at the queue according to a certain pattern, such as random (Poisson) arrivals, scheduled arrivals, or fixed intervals.

2. Service Process: Once customers reach the front of

the queue, they are served or processed by service providers or systems. The time taken to serve each customer is known as the service time.

3. Queue Length: The queue length refers to the number of customers waiting in line at a particular time.

4. Queue Discipline: Queue discipline determines the order in which customers are served from the waiting line. Common queue disciplines include first-come-first-served (FCFS), last-come-first-served (LCFS), and priority-based.

5. Queue Capacity: Queue capacity refers to the maximum number of customers that the queue can hold at any given time. If the queue reaches its capacity, additional customers may be turned away or asked to wait elsewhere.

6. Waiting Time: Waiting time is the time a customer spends waiting in the queue before receiving service.

7. Service Rate: The service rate represents the rate at which customers are served. It is the inverse of the average service time.

8. Arrival Rate: The arrival rate indicates the rate at which customers arrive at the queue. It is usually measured in customers per unit of time.

9. Utilization: The utilization of the system refers to the proportion of time the service providers are busy serving customers. It is the ratio of the arrival rate to the service rate.

Waiting lines can lead to customer frustration, especially when waiting times are long or when the service quality does not meet expectations. Managing waiting lines effectively is crucial for businesses and service providers to ensure customer satisfaction, optimize resource utilization, and maintain operational efficiency.

Various queuing models, such as M/M/1, M/M/c, M/G/1, and M/G/c, are used to analyze and optimize waiting lines, allowing organizations to make informed decisions for capacity planning, resource allocation, and service improvements. Additionally, managing customer expectations, providing entertainment or comfort during waiting, and implementing efficient service processes can contribute to a positive waiting experience and improved customer satisfaction.

WAITING LINE MANAGEMENT, also known as queuing management, involves the strategies and techniques employed to effectively handle waiting lines or queues in various settings, such as retail stores, service centers, healthcare facilities, and transportation hubs. The primary goal of waiting line management is to enhance customer satisfaction, optimize resource utilization, and improve overall operational efficiency.

Queue management deals with cases where the customer arrival is random; therefore, service rendered to them is also random.

A service organization can reduce cost and thus improve profitability by efficient queue management. A cost is associated with customer waiting in line and there is cost associated with adding new counters to reduce service time. Queue management looks to address this trade off and offer solutions to management.

Waiting Line Problems

Waiting in line is common phenomena in daily life, for example, banks have customers in line to get service of teller, cars queue up for re-filling, workers line up to access machine to complete their job. Therefore, **management needs to work on formulae, which will reduce wait time and create delighted customers without incurring an additional cost**. Generally, queue management problems are tradeoffs situation between cost of time spent in waiting v/s cost of additional capacity or machinery.

Finite and Infinite Population

In a waiting line scenario, there are cases of finite population of customers and infinite population of customers.

- **A finite population scenario** considers a fixed or limited size of customers visiting the service counter. It also assumes that customer once served will leave the line thus reducing overall population of customers.

However finite population model also considers a scenario where the customer after getting served will re-visit the service counter for re-service, leading to increase in finite population.

- **An infinite population theory** looks at a scenario where subtractions and addition of customer do not impact overall workability of the model.

Queuing System

Queuing systems, also known as waiting line systems or queuing theory, are mathematical models used to analyze and study the behavior of waiting lines or queues. Queuing systems are prevalent in various real-world scenarios where customers or entities wait for service or processing. Examples of queuing systems include lines at retail stores, banks, airports, call centers, healthcare facilities, and traffic congestion on highways.

Features / components of queuing systems:

1. Arrival Process: The arrival process refers to the pattern or distribution of customers or entities entering the queuing system. It can follow different patterns, such as Poisson arrivals (random), deterministic arrivals (fixed intervals), or scheduled

arrivals.

2. Service Process: The service process represents how customers or entities are served once they reach the front of the queue. The service times can vary depending on the complexity of the task, the resources available, and the service rate.

3. Queue Discipline: Queue discipline determines the order in which customers are served from the waiting line. Common queue disciplines include first-come-first-served (FCFS), last-come-first-served (LCFS), priority-based, and shortest remaining processing time (SRPT).

4. Queue Length: The queue length is the number of customers or entities waiting in the queue at a particular time.

5. Queue Capacity: Queue capacity refers to the maximum number of customers that the queue can hold at any given time.

6. Service Capacity: The service capacity represents the rate at which customers can be served, often measured as the number of customers served per unit of time.

Queuing theory allows businesses and service providers to analyze and optimize various aspects of queuing systems, such as:

- Waiting Times: Queuing theory helps calculate average waiting times and queue lengths, which are crucial for managing customer expectations.

- Service Utilization: It helps in determining the utilization of service resources (e.g., servers, agents) to avoid overloading or underutilization.

- Resource Allocation: Queuing theory assists in allocating resources effectively, such as determining the optimal number of servers or service points required to meet demand.

- Cost Analysis: By understanding queuing behavior, organizations can make cost-effective decisions related to staffing, service levels, and infrastructure.

- Performance Evaluation: Queuing theory allows organizations to evaluate the performance of their queuing systems, identify inefficiencies, and implement improvements.

- Forecasting: Using historical data and queuing models, businesses can forecast future queue lengths and waiting times to prepare for peak periods.

To solve problems related to queue management it is important to understand characteristics of the queue. Some common queue situations are waiting in line for service in super-market or banks, waiting for results from computer and waiting in line for bus or commuter rail.

General premise of queue theory is that there are limited resources for a given population of customers and addition of a new service line will increase the cost aspect to the business. A typical queue system has the following:

1. **Arrival Process:** As the name suggests an arrival process look at different components of customer arrival. Customer arrival could in single, batch or bulk, arrival as distribution of time, arrival in finite population or infinite population.

2. **Service Mechanism:** this looks at available resources for customer service, queue structure to avail the service and preemption of service. Underlining assumption here is that service time of customers is independent of arrival to the queue.

3. **Queue Characteristics:** this looks at selection of

customers from the queue for service. Generally, customer selection is through first come first served method, random or last in first out. As a result, customers leave if the queue is long, customer leave if they have waited too long or switch to faster serving queue.

Service Configuration

Another aspect of waiting line management is the service configuration. There are four types of service configuration, and they are as follows:

- Single Channel, Single Phase (e.g. ship yards and car wash)

- Single Channel, Multi Phase (e.g. bank tellers)

- Multi-Channel, Single Phase (e.g. separate queue of man and women for single ticket window)

- Multi-Channel, Multi Phase (e.g. Laundromat, where option of several washers and several dryers)

Capacity Planning and Queuing Models

Capacity planning in queuing networks involves analyzing and optimizing the resource capacity of interconnected queuing systems to meet demand efficiently. In queuing networks, customers move between multiple queues, and their service may involve passing through several service stations before completing their transactions. The capacity planning process in queueing networks is more complex than in single-queue systems, as it requires considering the interactions between different queues and their impact on overall system performance.

Methods of capacity planning using queuing models:

1. Little's Law: Little's Law is a fundamental principle in queuing theory that relates the average number of customers in the system (L), the average time a

customer spends in the system (W), and the average arrival rate (λ). It can be expressed as L = λ * W. This law helps in understanding the relationship between customer flow and waiting times and is often used as a starting point for capacity planning.

2. Queuing Network Models: Queuing network models, such as Jackson networks and closed queuing networks, are used to analyze queuing systems with multiple interconnected queues and service stations. These models help understand the impact of customer routing and system configurations on performance metrics. Capacity planning in queuing networks involves adjusting the number of servers or resources at each station to optimize overall system performance.

3. Utilization Analysis: Calculating the utilization (ρ) of each server or resource in the queuing system is a fundamental capacity planning method. Utilization is the ratio of the average service rate to the average arrival rate ($\rho = \lambda / \mu$). High utilization indicates potential bottlenecks, and capacity may need to be increased to prevent service congestion.

4. Sensitivity Analysis: Conducting sensitivity analysis involves testing the queuing model under different scenarios and varying input parameters. This helps identify critical factors that significantly affect capacity requirements. Sensitivity analysis helps in understanding how changes in arrival rates, service rates, or other parameters impact the system's performance.

5. Optimization Techniques: Optimization techniques, such as linear programming and numerical optimization methods, can be used to find the optimal allocation of resources to minimize waiting

times, reduce service congestion, and balance capacity across different queues or service stations.

6. Simulation: Simulation involves running computer-based simulations of the queuing system to observe its behavior under various conditions. Capacity planning through simulation allows for testing different resource allocation strategies and service configurations in a risk-free environment.

7. Queue Disciplines and Prioritization: Queue disciplines, such as first-come-first-served (FCFS) or priority-based queuing, can influence the flow of customers through the system. By adjusting queue disciplines or prioritizing certain customer segments, capacity planning can be fine-tuned to meet specific service level objectives.

8. Contingency Planning: Queuing models can be used to simulate scenarios during peak demand or unexpected events. Capacity planning involves developing contingency plans to handle temporary spikes in demand or system disruptions.

Analytical Queuing Models

Analytical Queuing Models

- A/B/K System
    - A = Arrival Process
    - B = Service Process
    - K = number of servers
- Where
- M = Exponential inter-arrival or service times (or Poisson arrival or service rates)
- D= Deterministic or constant service times
- G= General service times

Analytical queuing models, also known as mathematical queuing models or exact queuing models, are mathematical representations used to analyze the behavior of queuing systems. These models are based on queuing theory; a branch of operations research that deals with the study of waiting lines or queues. Analytical queuing models provide insights into key performance metrics, such as waiting times, queue lengths, and resource utilization, without the need for simulation or real-world data. They are particularly useful for understanding the theoretical properties of queuing systems and for making predictions under different scenarios. Here are some common analytical queuing models:

Analytical Formulas

- When the queue discipline is FCFS, analytical formulas have been derived for several different queuing models including the following:
  - *M/M/1*
  - *M/M/k*
  - *M/G/1*
  - *M/G/k* with blocked customers cleared
  - *M/M/1* with a finite calling population
- Analytical formulas are not available for all possible queuing systems. In this event, insights may be gained through a simulation of the system.

1. M/M/1 Model: The M/M/1 model represents a single-server queuing system with Poisson arrivals (M for exponential inter-arrival times) and exponential service times (M for exponential service times). It assumes an infinite queue capacity and a first-come-first-served (FCFS) queue discipline. This model is straightforward to analyze and provides closed-form solutions for key performance metrics such as average queue length, average waiting time, and server utilization.

2. M/M/c Model: The M/M/c model extends the M/M/1 model to include multiple servers (c servers) in the system. The arrival process and service times remain exponentially distributed. This model is suitable for analyzing systems with parallel service stations, such as call centers or manufacturing lines.

3. M/G/1 Model: The M/G/1 model represents a single-server queuing system with Poisson arrivals (M for exponential inter-arrival times) and general service

times (G for any probability distribution). Unlike M/M/1, the service times can follow any distribution. This model is more flexible in capturing real-world variability in service times but may require more complex analysis methods.

4. M/M/c/c Model (Erlang-C Model): The M/M/c/c model represents a queuing system with c servers and a finite queue capacity of c customers. It is commonly used in call centers and telecommunications to estimate the probability that a customer has to wait before being served (blocking probability).

5. M/M/c/K Model (Erlang-B Model): The M/M/c/K model represents a queuing system with c servers and a finite queue capacity of K customers. It is used to estimate the probability of a customer being blocked (denied service) due to queue capacity limitations.

6. M/D/1 Model: The M/D/1 model represents a single-server queuing system with Poisson arrivals (M for exponential inter-arrival times) and deterministic service times (D for constant service times). This model assumes that each service time is constant and known in advance.

7. A/B/k queueing system is an analytical queuing model that represents a queuing system with k servers, where the service times follow a general probability distribution with mean $1/B$. In this model, customer arrivals occur at a rate of λ (Poisson arrivals with a rate of λ), and the service times follow a general distribution with mean $1/B$. The A/B/k model is an extension of the M/G/k model, where M represents Poisson arrivals and G denotes a general service time distribution.

Key characteristics of the A/B/k queueing system:

Arrival Process: Customer arrivals follow a Poisson process with a rate of λ, indicating that the inter-arrival times between customers are exponentially distributed.

Service Time Distribution: Service times have a general distribution with a mean of $1/B$. This distribution could be any non-exponential distribution, such as uniform, normal, exponential, or phase-type distributions.

Number of Servers: The system has k identical servers that can serve customers concurrently.

Analyzing the A/B/k queueing system can be more complex than the M/M/k or M/G/k models, as the general service time distribution adds mathematical complexity. To calculate performance metrics for the A/B/k model, one typically employs various mathematical techniques, such as the Pollaczek-Khintchine formula or numerical methods.

Common performance metrics for the A/B/k queueing system include:

Average Queue Length (Lq): The average number of customers waiting in the queue.

Average Waiting Time (Wq): The average time a customer spends waiting in the queue before being served.

Average Response Time (W): The average time a customer spends in the system (waiting time + service time).

Server Utilization (ρ): The proportion of time the servers are busy serving customers.

Blocking Probability (Pb): The probability that a customer is blocked (denied service) due to a full system.

Capacity Planning Criteria

Capacity planning involves determining the appropriate level of resources required to handle customer demand efficiently and minimize waiting times. Several criteria are considered in capacity planning for waiting lines to ensure that the system operates optimally.

Capacity planning criteria:

1. Service Level Objectives: Define specific service level objectives, such as the target maximum waiting time, average waiting time, or queue length. These objectives help set performance benchmarks for the waiting line system.

2. Customer Demand Forecast: Accurately forecast customer demand patterns to understand peak periods and anticipate fluctuations in demand. Demand forecasting provides valuable information for determining the required capacity to meet customer needs effectively.

3. Utilization: Monitor and manage resource utilization to avoid underutilization, which incurs unnecessary costs, or overutilization, which results in increased waiting times and reduced service quality.

4. Queue Length: Analyze the average queue length or the proportion of time the queue is empty (queue length = 0). Long queues can lead to dissatisfied customers and potential business losses.

5. Waiting Time: Minimize average waiting time to improve customer satisfaction. Consider the trade-off between shorter waiting times and the cost of additional resources required to achieve this goal.

6. Service Rate: Assess the efficiency of service delivery by evaluating the average service rate or the number of customers served per unit of time.

7. Variability: Account for variability in arrival rates and service times. Queuing systems with high variability may require more capacity to handle fluctuations effectively.

8. Resource Constraints: Consider any physical, operational, or budgetary constraints that may limit the maximum capacity of the system.

CHAPTER 7

Service Supply Relationships

Service supply relationships refer to the connections and interactions between service providers and their suppliers.

Service supply relationship management is a systems approach that recognizes the customer-supplier duality found in the delivery of services. For services, customers are suppliers of significant inputs (i.e., minds, bodies, belongings, and information) to the process. Implications for management arise from the fact that service supply relationships are inherently bi-directional. Three important features of service supply relationship management are bi-directional optimization, management of productive capacity, and managing risk. Service supply relationship management incorporates customers into the knowledge management strategy of service companies to enhance the value and quality of the services provided.

In the context of service industries, service providers rely on various inputs, resources, and support from external entities to deliver their services effectively. These external entities are often referred to as service suppliers or vendors. Service supply relationships play a crucial role in ensuring the smooth functioning of service operations and meeting customer expectations.

Elements of service supply relationships:

- Service Inputs: Service providers require inputs or resources to deliver their services. These inputs may include raw materials, equipment, technology, software, trained personnel, and other necessary resources. Service providers establish relationships with suppliers to ensure the timely availability of these inputs.

- Outsourcing: In some cases, service providers outsource certain aspects of their operations to external vendors. Outsourcing allows service providers to focus on their core competencies while leveraging the specialized expertise of vendors for specific tasks or services.

- Service Level Agreements (SLAs): Service providers and suppliers often formalize their relationship through service level agreements (SLAs). SLAs define the expectations, responsibilities, performance metrics, and service quality standards that both parties must adhere to.

- Supply Chain Management: Service providers need to manage their supply chains effectively to ensure a seamless flow of inputs and resources. This involves coordinating with suppliers, managing inventory levels, and minimizing disruptions in the supply chain.

- Quality Assurance: Service supply relationships include mechanisms for quality assurance. Service providers must ensure that the inputs and resources they receive from suppliers meet the required standards and contribute to delivering high-quality services.

- Communication and Collaboration: Effective communication and collaboration between service providers and suppliers are essential for smooth operations. Regular communication ensures that both parties are aligned in their objectives and can address any issues promptly.

- Risk Management: Service providers need to identify and mitigate potential risks in their supply relationships. This includes assessing supplier reliability, backup plans for supply disruptions, and contingency strategies.

Supply Chain for Physical Goods

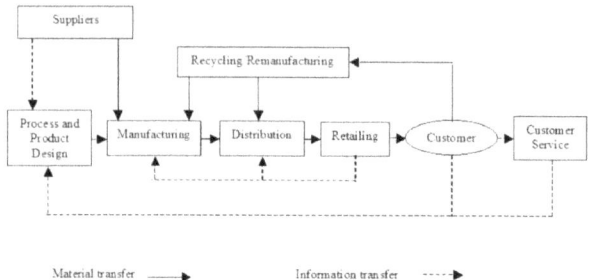

Customer-Supplier Duality in Service Supply Relationships (Hubs)

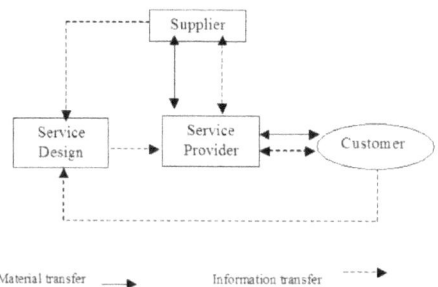

CUSTOMER-SUPPLIER DUALITY in service supply relationships refers to the concept that within a service ecosystem, each party can simultaneously act as a customer and a supplier to the other. This dynamic relationship exists in interconnected service networks where various entities collaborate to deliver a seamless service experience to the end customer. In such scenarios, organizations play multiple roles, both receiving services from others (as customers) and providing services to others (as suppliers) in a reciprocal manner.

Elements of customer-supplier duality:

1. Interdependent Service Providers: In service supply relationships, service providers often rely on inputs or services from other entities to deliver their services effectively. These providers, while acting as customers, procure necessary resources, expertise, or support from external suppliers to enhance their service delivery.

2. Value Co-creation: Within a service ecosystem, multiple organizations collaborate to co-create value for the end customer. Each organization's services contribute to the overall customer experience. This value co-creation involves a back-and-forth exchange of services between providers, leading to customer-supplier duality.

3. Reciprocal Relationships: The interactions between service providers are not unidirectional. Instead, they involve mutual exchange and collaboration. Organizations might serve as suppliers to one party while being a customer to another party, creating a network of reciprocal relationships.

4. Service Networks and Chains: Service supply relationships often form complex networks or chains, with one organization's service acting as an input for another. These interconnected relationships help organizations tap into specialized expertise and resources from various partners, leading to enhanced service capabilities.

5. Service Symbiosis: The concept of customer-supplier duality emphasizes that service providers within the ecosystem mutually benefit from each other's offerings. The synergy between different

organizations enhances the collective ability to deliver value to the end customer.

6. Importance of Collaboration: In such service ecosystems, collaboration and effective communication are crucial for maintaining a smooth flow of services and resources. Organizations need to align their objectives and work together to ensure seamless service delivery.

MANAGERIAL IMPLICATIONS OF BIDIRECTIONAL RELATIONSHIPS

Bidirectional service supply relationships refer to service supply relationships in which the flow of services and resources occurs in both directions between two or more parties. In these relationships, each party acts as both a customer and a supplier to the other, creating a reciprocal exchange of services, inputs, or support. This bidirectional flow is characteristic of interconnected service networks or ecosystems, where various entities collaborate to deliver a comprehensive service experience. Here are some key features and implications of bidirectional service supply relationships:

Bidirectional relationships in business, including bidirectional service supply relationships, have several managerial implications that organizations need to consider to effectively navigate and leverage these relationships. Here are some key managerial implications:

1. Enhanced Collaboration: Bidirectional relationships require a high level of collaboration and communication between parties. Managers should foster a culture of open communication and cooperation to ensure seamless information sharing and coordination among teams.

2. Focus on Mutual Benefits: Emphasize mutual benefits and value co-creation within bidirectional

relationships. Managers should work towards identifying win-win scenarios where both parties gain value from the exchange of services or resources.

3. Strategic Alliances: Bidirectional relationships often involve strategic alliances between organizations. Managers need to carefully assess potential partners and establish clear objectives, roles, and responsibilities to ensure the success of the alliance.

4. Relationship Management: Effective relationship management is crucial in bidirectional relationships. Managers should monitor the health of the relationships, address any conflicts or issues promptly, and seek opportunities to strengthen ties with partners.

5. Flexibility and Adaptability: Bidirectional relationships may require organizations to be flexible and adaptable to changes in market conditions or partner needs. Managers should be prepared to adjust strategies and processes as necessary to accommodate evolving circumstances.

6. Trust Building: Building and maintaining trust is essential in bidirectional relationships. Managers should foster an environment of trust and transparency to strengthen collaboration and foster long-term partnerships.

7. Performance Metrics: Establishing appropriate performance metrics and key performance indicators (KPIs) can help track the success and effectiveness of bidirectional relationships. These metrics can include customer satisfaction, efficiency gains, and overall business performance.

8. Risk Management: Bidirectional relationships introduce certain risks, such as dependency on

partners or potential conflicts of interest. Managers should develop risk management strategies to mitigate these risks and ensure business continuity.

9. Resource Optimization: Bidirectional relationships can lead to resource optimization, as organizations can leverage each other's strengths and expertise. Managers should identify opportunities to maximize resource utilization and reduce redundancies.

Single-Level Bidirectional Service Supply Relationship

Service Category	Customer-Supplier	>*Input* Output>	Service Provider
Minds	Student	>Mind Knowledge>	Professor
Bodies	Patient	>Tooth Filling>	Dentist
Belongings	Investor	>Money Interest>	Bank
Information	Client	>Documents 1040>	Tax Preparer

Two-Level Bidirectional Service Supply Relationship

Service Category	Customer -Supplier	>*Input Output*>	Service Provider	>*Input Output*>	Provider's Supplier
Minds	Patient	>Disturbed Treated>	Therapist	>Prescription Drugs>	Pharmacy
Bodies	Patient	>Blood Diagnosis>	Physician	>Sample Test Result>	Lab
Belongings	Driver	>Car Repaired>	Garage	>Engine Rebuilt>	Machine Shop
Information	Home Buyer	>Property Loan>	Mortgage Company	>Location Clear Title>	Title Search

SOURCES OF VALUE IN SERVICE SUPPLY RELATIONSHIPS

- Bi-directional Optimization
- Managing Productive Capacity
  - Transfer: make knowledge available (e.g. web based FAQ database)
  - Replacement: substitute technology for server (e.g. digital blood pressure device)
  - Embellishment: enable self-service by teaching (e.g. change surgical dressing)
- Management of Perishability

Impact of Service Supply Relationships

Element or Link	Before	After
Channel Structure	Functional silos	Process orientation
Service Recipient	Passive	Active as a co-producer
Channel Integration	Vertical (own the channel to integrate)	Virtual (IT and other mechanism permit integration without ownership)
Flow of Service	Available waiting for demand	Activated upon demand
Flow of Information (upstream)	Pull: manual reporting of demand data results in delayed management response.	Push: high level of connectivity and transparency with fast or instantaneous access to most recent demand data.
Flow of Information (downstream)	Little or no knowledge of resource deployment	Real-time tracking and dispatching
Business Processes	Predominantly in-house; locally optimized for efficiency	In-house for key processes, others out-sourced for flexibility; integrated and synchronized to match supply with demand
Demand Management	Limited to use of appointments and reservations.	Proactive involving customer in scheduling to achieve bi-directional optimization

Impact of Service Supply Relationships

Element or Link	Before	After
Capacity Management	Limited to use of part-time employees	Creative use of cross-trained employees, outsourcing, and customer self-service.
Facilitating Goods	High; in anticipation of demand	Lower; owing to process transparency
Service Delivery	Inflexible; standardized and impersonal	Flexible; personable with customization possible.
Routing and scheduling	Static; fixed daily schedules	Dynamic; based on system connectivity and process visibility
New Service Design	Marketing initiatives based on firm's perception of customer needs	Virtual value chain design with customer data base information driving new services
Pricing	Fixed	Variable; yield management promotes off-peak demand and avoid idle capacity
International Operations	Focus on domestic market	Global reach with Internet

OUTSOURCING SERVICES AND ITS MANAGERIAL CONSIDERATIONS

Outsourcing services is a strategic decision made by

190

organizations to delegate certain non-core business functions or tasks to external service providers. By outsourcing, companies can focus on their core competencies, reduce costs, access specialized expertise, and improve overall efficiency. However, successful outsourcing requires careful planning and management.

Outsourcing Services

- *Benefits*
  - allows the firm to focus on its core competence
  - service is cheaper to outsource than perform in-house
  - provides access to latest technology
  - leverage benefits of supplier economy of scale
- *Risks*
  - loss of direct control of quality
  - jeopardizes employee loyalty
  - exposure to data security and customer privacy
  - dependence on one supplier compromises future negotiation leverage
  - additional coordination expense and delays
  - atrophy of in-house capability to perform service

Outsourcing Process

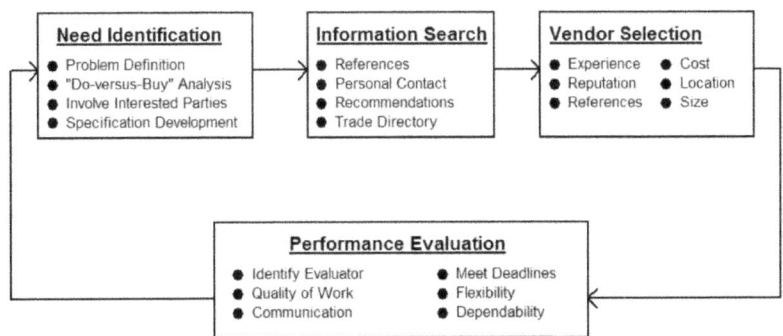

Taxonomy for Outsourcing Business Services

| | | Importance of Service | |
		Low	*High*
Focus	*Property*	**Facility Support:** -Laundry -Janitorial -Waste disposal	**Equipment Support:** -Repairs -Maintenance -Product testing
of	*People*	**Employee Support:** -Food service -Plant security -Temporary personnel	**Employee Development:** -Training -Education -Medical care
Service	*Process*	**Facilitator:** -Bookkeeping -Travel booking -Packaged software	**Professional:** -Advertising -Public relations -Legal

Outsourcing Considerations

Focus on Property

Facility Support Service

- Low cost
- Identify responsible party to evaluate performance
- Precise specifications can be written

Equipment Support Service

- Experience and reputation of vendor
- Availability of vendor for emergency response
- Designate person to make service call and to check that service is satisfactory

Outsourcing Considerations

Focus on People

Employee Support Service

- Contact vendor clients for references
- Specifications prepared with end user input
- Evaluate performance on a periodic basis

Employee Development Service

- Experience with particular industry important
- Involve high levels of management in vendor identification and selection
- Contact vendor clients for references
- Use employees to evaluate vendor performance

Outsourcing Considerations

Focus on Process

Facilitator Service

- Knowledge of alternate vendors important
- Involve end user in vendor identification
- References or third party evaluations useful
- Have user write detailed specifications

Professional Service

- Involve high level management in vendor identification and selection
- Reputation and experience very important
- Performance evaluation by top management

Managerial considerations for outsourcing services:

1. Defining Objectives: Clearly define the objectives

and expected outcomes of outsourcing. Determine which services or processes are suitable for outsourcing and align them with the organization's strategic goals.

2. Vendor Selection: Carefully select the right outsourcing vendor based on their expertise, track record, financial stability, and cultural fit. Conduct due diligence to ensure the vendor can meet the organization's requirements and service levels.

3. Service Level Agreements (SLAs): Establish comprehensive SLAs that clearly outline the scope of services, performance metrics, responsibilities, and penalties for non-compliance. SLAs help set expectations and ensure service quality.

4. Risk Management: Identify potential risks associated with outsourcing and develop risk management strategies. Address issues like data security, intellectual property protection, regulatory compliance, and vendor performance.

5. Communication and Collaboration: Maintain open and transparent communication with the outsourcing partner. Regularly review performance, address concerns, and foster a collaborative relationship to enhance service delivery.

6. Cost Analysis: Conduct a thorough cost analysis to compare the expenses of outsourcing with in-house operations. Consider both direct and indirect costs, including transition costs and potential hidden costs.

7. Change Management: Prepare the organization for the outsourcing transition by communicating the reasons, benefits, and implications of outsourcing to employees. Address any resistance to change and provide necessary training and support.

8. Data Protection and Confidentiality: Ensure that proper data protection measures are in place to safeguard sensitive information shared with the outsourcing partner. Sign confidentiality agreements to protect intellectual property and proprietary information.

9. Flexibility and Scalability: Ensure that the outsourcing arrangement allows for flexibility and scalability to accommodate changing business needs and future growth.

10. Performance Monitoring: Regularly monitor the performance of the outsourcing vendor against the SLAs and key performance indicators (KPIs). Conduct periodic performance reviews and make adjustments if needed.

11. Exit Strategy: Develop an exit strategy in case the outsourcing relationship needs to be terminated or transferred to another vendor. Consider data retrieval, knowledge transfer, and potential legal and financial implications.

CHAPTER 8

Growth and Globalization of Services

The growth and globalization of services have been significant trends in the global economy over the past few decades. Traditionally, the focus was on the manufacturing and agricultural sectors, but the rise of services has reshaped the global economic landscape.

Meaning of Service Globalization

Services are intangible and perishable benefits offered to consumers to satisfy their needs and wants. These services can be marketed across national borders, making them exportable. **The phenomenon of a service provider catering to consumers in other nations is known as Service Globalization.**

Currently, the value of services in global trade is slightly above 20 percent, and it is expected to grow further due to various factors facilitating its spread, with Information Technology (IT) being one of the most significant contributors. While almost all services can be exported, the World Trade Organization (WTO) identifies **four service exportation models:**

1. Marketing a service across national borders, for example, selling air tickets.

2. Consumers crossing the border to avail a service, such as seeking medical treatment in another country or tourists visiting a country for recreational purposes.

3. Organizations opening subsidiaries in foreign countries to market services, like a restaurant opening branches in new countries.

4. Professionals sent by organizations to deliver

services across borders, like a consultancy organization sending an expatriate to another country for service delivery.

Statistically, only the first two models of global services are accounted for in the globalization of services. However, it is important to note that most of the global service value is generated through the third model. Today, the service sector worldwide is witnessing a revolution and driving an intangible economy structure. Professional services like banking and various IT-enabled services are precursors to this unprecedented boom in the global delivery model.

Steps to Prepare for Globalization:

Service Globalization refers to increased competition between service providers in the international market due to lower market entry barriers and larger growth opportunities.

i) Secure a strong domestic market share: The organization should focus on establishing a robust presence in the domestic market. To achieve this, they need to be perceived as the player who better understands local tastes, preferences, and relationships compared to their competitors.

ii) Define a clear vision for target customers: Once the organization has solidified its position in the domestic market, it can plan a strategic approach to enter the global market. This involves defining a clear vision for target customers they are passionate about serving.

iii) Develop a global service production and distribution network: The defined vision will serve as a guiding force to develop a global service production and distribution network. This means taking advantage of economic opportunities in various regions and countries to expand their service offerings internationally.

Preparing for globalization requires careful planning and execution. By building a strong domestic foundation, identifying target markets, and establishing a global network, service organizations can position themselves for success in the competitive global marketplace.

Domestic growth and expansion strategies

Domestic growth and expansion strategies refer to the methods and approaches that businesses use to increase their market share, revenues, and presence within their home country. These strategies are designed to capitalize on the existing market opportunities and resources within the country of operation.

Domestic Growth & Expansion Strategies

	Single Service	Multiservice
Single Location	Focused service: • Dental practice • Retail store • Family restaurant	Clustered service: • Stanford University • Mayo Clinic • USAA Insurance
Multisite	Focused network: • Federal Express • McDonald's • Red Roof Inns	Diversified network: • NationsBank • American Express • Accenture

FOCUSED SERVICE, FOCUSED NETWORK, CLUSTERED SERVICE, DIVERSIFIED NETWORK

• Focused Service: Focused service refers to a business strategy where a company concentrates its efforts and resources on providing a specific set of services to a well-defined target market or customer segment. Rather than trying to appeal to a broad audience, the company focuses on meeting the specialized needs of a particular group of customers. This approach allows the company to become highly skilled and efficient in delivering those specific services and better cater to the unique demands of their chosen market.

• Focused Network: A focused network is a network structure or partnership arrangement in which companies or organizations come together to collaborate and provide specialized services to a particular market or industry. These networks are formed to leverage the expertise of each member organization to serve the specific needs of their shared target audience. By pooling their resources and capabilities, the participants in a focused network can offer comprehensive solutions and gain a competitive advantage in the market they aim to serve.

• Clustered Service: Clustered service refers to the geographical concentration of similar or related service providers in a particular area. This clustering can occur naturally due to factors like industry trends, access to resources, or proximity to target customers. When multiple service providers in the same sector or niche operate in close proximity, it creates a cluster of related businesses, which often leads to benefits such as enhanced collaboration, knowledge sharing, and economies of scale. For customers, a service cluster provides a wide range of options and easy access to specialized services.

• Diversified Network: A diversified network involves an interconnected structure of various companies or organizations that offer a wide range of services across multiple industries or markets. Unlike a focused network that concentrates on serving a specific segment, a diversified network spans different sectors, allowing each member organization to tap into various markets and customer bases. This strategy enables the network to adapt to changing market conditions and take advantage of opportunities in different areas.

Franchising:

Franchising is a business model and a method of distribution that allows individuals or entities (franchisees) to own and operate a business using the established brand, products, and services of an existing company (franchisor). In a franchise arrangement, the franchisor grants the franchisee the right to use its business model, trademarks, and other intellectual property, while the franchisee pays fees or royalties and agrees to operate the business according to the franchisor's established standards and guidelines.

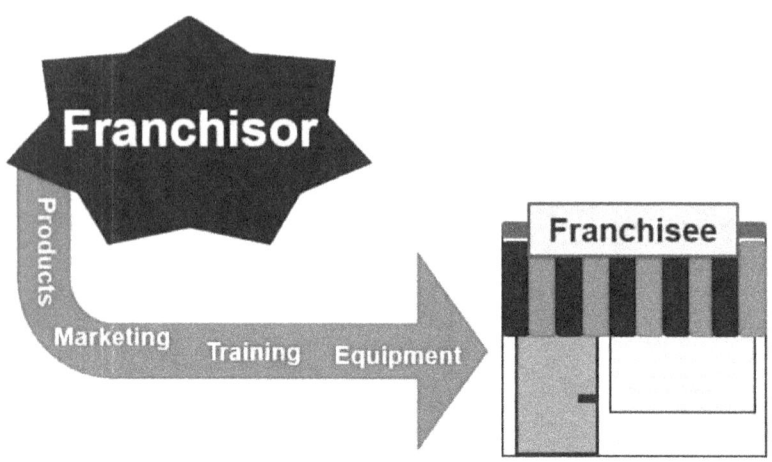

Franchising

Franchising is the arrangement between two parties where the first party (the franchiser) grants the second party (the franchisee) the right to utilize its business processes, produce and market a service or goods or simply use its trademark. The franchiser collects a one-time payable franchisee fee as well as a percentage of sales from the franchiser.

Advantages	Disadvantages
• Access To Better Talent	• Less Control Over Managers
• Easy Expansion Capital	• A Weaker Core Community
• Minimized Growth Risk	• Innovation Challenges

Franchise agreement typically includes:

1. Brand and Trademarks: The franchisee gains the right to use the franchisor's brand name, logos, trademarks, and trade dress, which are often well-known and carry customer recognition.

2. Business Model: The franchisee receives access to the franchisor's proven business model, operational systems, and processes. This includes training on how to run the business effectively.

3. Support and Training: Franchisors usually provide initial training to the franchisee and ongoing support, such as marketing assistance, operational guidance, and help with day-to-day challenges.

4. Territory: Franchise agreements may specify an exclusive or non-exclusive territory within which the franchisee can operate. This helps prevent direct competition with other franchisees of the same brand.

5. Fees and Royalties: Franchisees typically pay upfront fees for the right to become a franchisee, as well as ongoing royalties based on a percentage of their revenues or a fixed amount.

Advantages of Franchising:

1. Established Brand: Franchisees benefit from the use of an already established and recognized brand, which can attract customers and reduce the need for extensive marketing efforts.

2. Proven Business Model: Franchisors have already tested and refined their business models, reducing the risks associated with starting a business from scratch.

3. Training and Support: Franchisees receive training and ongoing support from the franchisor, helping them navigate challenges and improve their operations.

4. Economies of Scale: Franchisees can take advantage of the collective purchasing power and economies of scale of the entire franchise network, leading to potential cost savings.

5. Entrepreneurial Opportunities: Franchising allows individuals to own and operate their own businesses while benefiting from the support and resources of a

larger organization.

Disadvantages of Franchising:

1. Initial Costs: Franchisees may face significant upfront costs, including franchise fees, training expenses, and purchasing required equipment or inventory.

2. Ongoing Fees: Franchisees must pay ongoing royalties and other fees to the franchisor, impacting their profit margins.

3. Less Flexibility: Franchisees must adhere to the franchisor's guidelines and standards, limiting their ability to make independent business decisions.

4. Risk of Brand Damage: The actions of one franchisee can impact the reputation of the entire franchise network, potentially affecting other franchisees.

Nature

The nature of franchising revolves around a unique business relationship between two parties: the franchisor and the franchisee. This business model allows the franchisee (an individual or entity) to operate a business using the established brand, products, and business systems of the franchisor. The franchisor grants the franchisee the right to use its intellectual property, business model, and ongoing support in exchange for certain fees and adherence to established standards.

Nature of franchising:

1. Partnership: Franchising creates a partnership between the franchisor and the franchisee. While they are separate legal entities, they work together to expand the brand's presence and market share.

2. Brand and Intellectual Property: The franchisor owns the brand, trademarks, logos, and other

intellectual property associated with the business. The franchisee gains the right to use these assets, leveraging the established reputation and customer recognition of the brand.

3. Business Model and Operations: The franchisor provides the franchisee with a proven and standardized business model, including operational processes, marketing strategies, and quality control guidelines.

4. Training and Support: Franchisors typically offer initial training to franchisees and ongoing support throughout the franchise agreement. This support may include assistance with marketing, site selection, product sourcing, and operational challenges.

5. Fees and Royalties: Franchisees pay upfront fees to become part of the franchise system and ongoing royalties based on a percentage of their sales. These fees contribute to the continued support and development of the franchise network.

6. Standardization and Consistency: Franchising thrives on standardization and consistency. Franchisees are expected to follow the franchisor's guidelines and maintain a consistent customer experience across all franchise locations.

7. Geographic Exclusivity: In some cases, franchise agreements may include geographic exclusivity, meaning that the franchisee has the sole right to operate in a specific territory.

8. Legal Agreement: Franchising involves a legal contract, the franchise agreement, which outlines the rights, responsibilities, and obligations of both the franchisor and the franchisee.

9. Growth and Expansion: Franchising provides a way for the franchisor to expand its brand and business without shouldering the full cost and risk of opening and operating new locations. For franchisees, it offers an opportunity to start a business with the support of an established brand.

10. Risk and Rewards: While franchising offers benefits such as brand recognition and support, it also comes with risks. The success of a franchisee depends on various factors, including local market conditions and their ability to adhere to the franchisor's standards.

Benefits to Franchisee

Franchising offers several benefits to the franchisee, making it an attractive business opportunity for individuals or entities looking to start their own business. Here are some of the key benefits to the franchisee:

1. Established Brand and Customer Base: As a franchisee, you get to operate under an established and recognized brand. This brand recognition can attract customers and provide a head start in building a customer base compared to starting a business from scratch.

2. Proven Business Model: Franchisors have already tested and refined their business model, so as a franchisee, you have access to a proven and successful way of doing business. This reduces the risk associated with starting a new venture and increases the likelihood of success.

3. Training and Support: Franchisors typically provide comprehensive training to franchisees. This includes initial training to help you understand the business operations, marketing strategies, and customer

service standards. Ongoing support is also available to help you navigate challenges and maintain consistency.

4. Marketing and Advertising Assistance: Franchisees benefit from national or regional marketing campaigns run by the franchisor. This collective marketing effort can increase brand visibility and attract customers to your local franchise location.

5. Economies of Scale: As part of a larger franchise network, you may enjoy cost advantages due to bulk purchasing power. This can lead to reduced costs for inventory, equipment, and supplies.

6. Reduced Risk: The success rate of franchises tends to be higher than that of independent startups. The established brand, business model, and support from the franchisor contribute to a lower risk of failure.

7. Site Selection and Lease Negotiation: The franchisor often assists with site selection and lease negotiation for the franchise location. This expertise can help you find a suitable and strategic location for your business.

8. Continuous Innovation: Franchisors continuously invest in research and development to improve their products and services. As a franchisee, you can benefit from these ongoing innovations and updates.

9. Network of Peers: Being part of a franchise network provides access to a community of fellow franchisees. This network can offer valuable support, advice, and best practices sharing.

10. Quick Start-Up: Franchising allows you to get your business up and running relatively quickly. With an established model and support from the franchisor, you can focus on implementing the business rather

than starting from scratch.

11. Management Training: Franchisors often provide training in management and leadership skills, helping franchisees to effectively run their business and manage employees.

Issues in Franchising

While franchising offers numerous benefits, it is not without its challenges and potential issues. Franchisees and franchisors may encounter various problems throughout the course of their business relationship. Some of the common issues in franchising include:

1. Franchise Agreement Disputes: Disputes may arise between franchisees and franchisors over contract terms, territorial rights, royalty payments, marketing funds, and other obligations outlined in the franchise agreement.

2. Lack of Autonomy: Franchisees must operate their businesses within the guidelines set by the franchisor. This can sometimes lead to a lack of autonomy and limited decision-making power for franchisees, which may be frustrating for some entrepreneurs.

3. Initial Costs and Ongoing Fees: Franchisees often have to pay significant upfront costs to join a franchise system, including franchise fees and other expenses. Additionally, ongoing royalty payments and marketing fund contributions can impact the franchisee's profitability.

4. Profitability and Return on Investment (ROI): While franchising may offer a proven business model, success is not guaranteed. The profitability and ROI of a franchise can vary based on factors such as location, local market conditions, competition, and

the franchisee's management skills.

5. Market Saturation: In some markets, there might be an oversaturation of franchise outlets for a particular brand or industry. This can lead to intense competition among franchisees and potentially impact sales and profitability.

6. Quality Control and Brand Reputation: The actions of one franchisee can reflect on the entire franchise brand. Maintaining consistent quality standards and brand reputation across all franchise locations is crucial, and a single poorly managed outlet can negatively affect the brand as a whole.

7. Training and Support: The level of training and support provided by the franchisor can vary. Some franchisees may feel that they need more guidance or assistance than what is offered.

8. Changes to the Franchise System: Franchisors may make changes to the business model, products, or services over time. While these changes may be intended to improve the overall system, they can sometimes create challenges or conflicts for franchisees.

9. Renewal and Termination Issues: Franchise agreements typically have a set term, and renewal is subject to certain conditions. Disputes can arise during the renewal process, and termination of the agreement may occur if franchisees fail to meet performance or compliance standards.

GLOBALIZATION OF SERVICES:

The globalization of services refers to the increasing integration and expansion of service-based industries across national borders. It is a result of advancements in technology, improved communication networks, liberalization of trade, and the removal of barriers to international business. Just as goods and products have been traded globally for centuries, services are now crossing borders at an accelerating pace.

Aspects of the globalization of services include:

1. Cross-Border Trade: Service providers now offer their services to customers in different countries, often facilitated by digital platforms and the internet. For example, consulting firms, software developers, call centers, and creative agencies can provide services to clients worldwide without the need for physical presence.

2. Outsourcing and Offshoring: Globalization has led to the outsourcing and offshoring of services to countries with lower labor costs and specialized expertise. Companies in developed countries may outsource certain services, such as customer support or data processing, to countries where labor is more affordable.

3. Offshore Service Centers: Many companies set up offshore service centers in other countries to handle specific functions. These centers benefit from cost savings while maintaining service quality and efficiency.

4. Knowledge Economy: The globalization of services has contributed to the emergence of a knowledge-based economy. Intellectual capital, expertise, and innovation are becoming essential drivers of economic growth and competitiveness.

5. International Collaboration: Globalization has facilitated collaboration and partnerships between service providers in different countries. Companies may collaborate to access new markets, share

knowledge, and combine resources to offer comprehensive services.

6. Movement of Skilled Labor: Skilled professionals, such as doctors, engineers, IT specialists, and researchers, may move across borders to offer their services to foreign clients or work for multinational organizations.

7. Digital Platforms and E-Commerce: The rise of digital platforms and e-commerce has made it easier for service providers to reach customers in distant locations. This has expanded the potential reach of service businesses beyond traditional geographical boundaries.

GENERIC INTERNATIONAL STRATEGIES

Generic international strategies are broad approaches that companies can adopt when expanding their operations into international markets. These strategies are not specific to any particular industry or company but provide a framework for businesses to navigate the complexities of international markets. There are three main generic international strategies

1. Global Strategy: The global strategy aims to achieve standardization and consistency in products, marketing, and operations across all international markets. Companies that pursue a global strategy treat the world as a single, integrated market and develop standardized products that can be sold with minimal modifications globally. They focus on economies of scale, cost efficiency, and centralized decision-making to achieve a competitive advantage. Key features of a global strategy include:

- Centralized production and distribution facilities to achieve economies of scale.

- Uniform branding and marketing messages to create

a consistent global image.

- Limited product customization to reduce costs.
- High emphasis on research and development to create standardized products.
- Global sourcing of raw materials and components to minimize costs.

2. Multinational Strategy: A multinational strategy, also known as a multidomestic strategy, emphasizes local responsiveness and adaptation to the unique characteristics of each international market. Companies that adopt this strategy tailor their products, marketing, and operations to suit the preferences and needs of individual countries or regions. The goal is to achieve a high level of customer satisfaction by customizing products and services to meet local demands. Key features of a multinational strategy include:

- Decentralized decision-making to adapt to local market conditions and customer preferences.
- Customization of products and services to address cultural, regulatory, and consumer differences.
- Local marketing and branding strategies to resonate with specific markets.
- Collaboration with local partners and joint ventures to gain local market knowledge and access.

3. Transnational Strategy: The transnational strategy seeks to strike a balance between global standardization and local responsiveness. Companies that pursue a transnational strategy aim to achieve global efficiency while remaining flexible enough to adapt to local market conditions. They integrate the benefits of both the global and multinational strategies to create a

cohesive international presence. Key features of a transnational strategy include:

- Standardization of core products and processes to achieve economies of scale and efficiency.

- Adaptation of products and marketing to cater to local preferences and needs.

- Global coordination of operations to leverage resources and knowledge.

- Decentralized decision-making to accommodate regional differences and customer demands.

- Continuous learning and knowledge sharing across international operations.

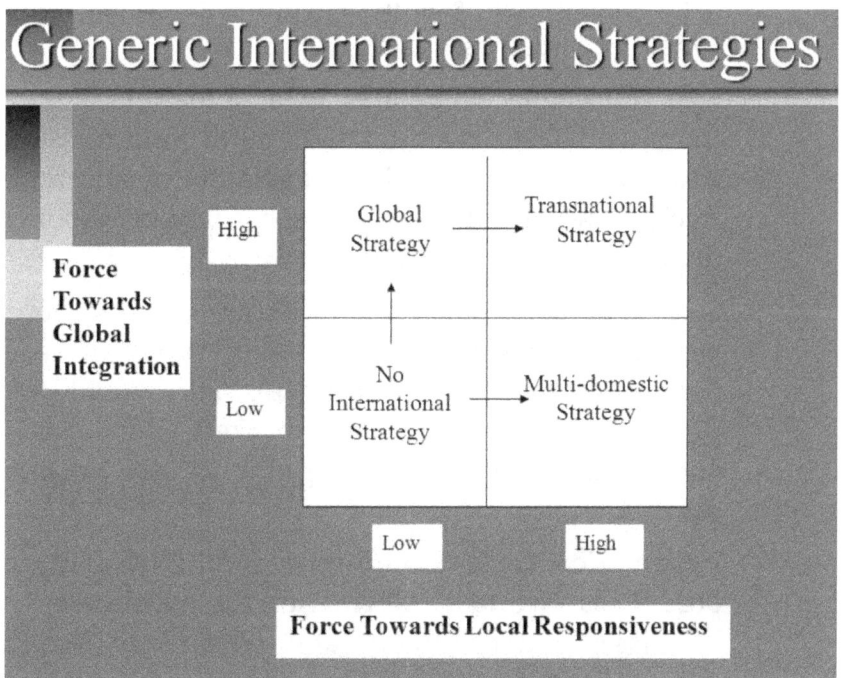

Nature of Borderless World

Borderless world is a concept of globalization where the goods, services, technology, information, capital flow through the borders from one nation to other.

The concept of a "borderless world" refers to a hypothetical or idealized global condition where national borders and barriers to international interactions and movements have significantly diminished or disappeared. It envisions a world where people, goods, services, information, and ideas flow freely across geographical boundaries without the constraints of traditional borders.

The nature of a borderless world is characterized by several key elements:

1. Global Interconnectedness: In a borderless world, countries, economies, and societies are highly interconnected and interdependent. Advances in transportation, communication, and technology have facilitated seamless connections between people and businesses worldwide.

2. Free Movement of People: In a borderless world, there would be fewer restrictions on immigration and emigration, allowing people to move more freely between countries for work, study, or personal reasons.

3. Free Trade and Global Markets: Borderless conditions would encourage free trade and the removal of trade barriers such as tariffs and quotas. This would lead to the development of global markets where goods and services could be exchanged more easily across countries.

4. Information and Communication Flow: In a borderless world, information and ideas can be disseminated rapidly and effortlessly across the globe, thanks to advanced communication technologies and the internet.

Planning Transnational Operations

Planning transnational operations requires a strategic approach that balances the need for global integration with local responsiveness. Transnational operations involve conducting business across national borders while effectively adapting to the unique characteristics and demands of different markets. Here are key steps to consider when planning transnational operations:

1. Market Research and Analysis: Conduct thorough market research to understand the target countries' economic, cultural, regulatory, and competitive landscapes. Identify market opportunities, consumer preferences, and potential challenges that may affect your business.

2. Define Global Strategy and Objectives: Establish clear global objectives for your transnational operations. Determine whether your focus is on global efficiency, local adaptation, or a combination of both (transnational strategy). Align these objectives with your overall corporate strategy.

3. Develop Standardization and Customization Plans: Identify core aspects of your products, services, and processes that can be standardized globally to achieve economies of scale. Simultaneously, devise strategies to customize offerings to cater to local needs and preferences.

4. Form Cross-Functional Teams: Assemble cross-functional teams that bring together expertise from different regions and disciplines. These teams can help develop strategies that consider both global and local perspectives.

5. Foster Global Collaboration: Promote collaboration and knowledge sharing among various business units and regional teams. Facilitate open communication channels to exchange best practices

and innovations across borders.

6. Ensure Regulatory Compliance: Comply with local laws, regulations, and industry standards in each country of operation. Adherence to local requirements is crucial to avoid legal and operational complications.

GLOBAL SERVICE STRATEGIES

Global service strategies refer to the approaches and plans that companies adopt to expand their service offerings and operations in international markets. These strategies aim to capitalize on global opportunities, address cross-border challenges, and create a competitive advantage in the global marketplace.

Global Service Strategies

- Multi-country expansion – Replicating a service in more than one country, often with little adaptation
- Importing customers – Attracting customers to an existing site rather than building overseas.
- Following your customer – Expanding overseas to serve existing customers with multinational operations
- Service offshoring – Outsourcing of activities internationally, often to reduce cost
- Beating the clock – Using service locations around the globe to achieve 24/7 service

Considerations in Selecting a Global Service Strategy

Globalization Factors	Global Service Strategies				
	Multicountry Expansion	Importing Customers	Follow Your Customers	Service Offshoring	Beating the Clock
Customer Contact	Train local workers	Develop foreign language & cultural sensitivity skills	Develop foreign customers	Specialize in back-office office service components	Provide extended hours of service
Customization	Usually a standard service	Strategic opportunity	Re-prototype locally	Quality and coordination	More need for reliability & coordination
Complexity	Usually routine	Strategic opportunity	Modify operations	Opportunity for focus	Time compression
Information Intensity	Satellite network	On site advantage	Move experienced managers	Training investments	Exploit opportunity
Cultural Adaptation	Modify service	Accommodate foreign guests	Could be necessary to achieve scale	Cultural understanding	Common language necessary
Labor Intensity	Reduced labor costs	Increased labor costs	Hire local personnel	Reduced labor costs	Reduced labor costs
Other	Government restrictions	Logistics management	Inadequate infrastructure	Home office employee morale	Capital investments

• Multi-country Expansion: Multi-country expansion involves establishing service operations or offices in multiple countries simultaneously. The company aims to tap into diverse international markets and expand its global presence. This strategy allows the company to cater directly to local customers in each country, offering customized services that suit their unique needs and preferences. Multi-country expansion often requires a significant investment in resources, talent, and infrastructure, but it can lead to increased market share and access to a broader customer base.

• Importing Customers: The "Importing Customers" strategy entails serving international customers from a central location, often the company's home country. In this approach, customers from various countries are targeted and served remotely without establishing a physical presence in each market. It leverages technology and digital platforms to deliver services globally. This strategy is suitable when the company's services can be effectively provided from a centralized location and when there is a demand from customers in multiple countries.

• Follow Your Customers: The "Follow Your Customers" strategy involves expanding service operations to new countries based on the movement and needs of existing customers. If a company's key customers or client base is expanding into specific international markets, the company may decide to follow its customers and establish a presence in those countries to continue providing services to them. This strategy ensures that the company maintains a close relationship with its existing customers and capitalizes on new opportunities in the markets where they are present.

• Service Offshoring: Service offshoring refers to relocating certain service functions or operations to foreign countries, often with lower labor costs or specialized skills. By offshoring some services, companies can reduce operational expenses while maintaining service quality. This strategy allows the company to access a global talent pool, optimize resource allocation, and stay competitive in the global market.

• Beating the Clock: The "Beating the Clock" strategy focuses on providing time-sensitive services efficiently and quickly. Companies adopting this strategy emphasize speed and responsiveness in service delivery to meet urgent customer demands or strict deadlines. Industries such as logistics, emergency services, healthcare, and consulting often employ this strategy to address critical situations or time-critical tasks.

Abhishek Sharma
Manish Sharma

2023